MESSAGES OF HOPE -- AFFIRMATIONS TO EMPOWER YOUR LIFE

Premier Edition Published in 2015 in the United States of America

WWW.MYDOVESONG.COM

ISBN-13: 978-0615977829

ISBN-10: 0615977820

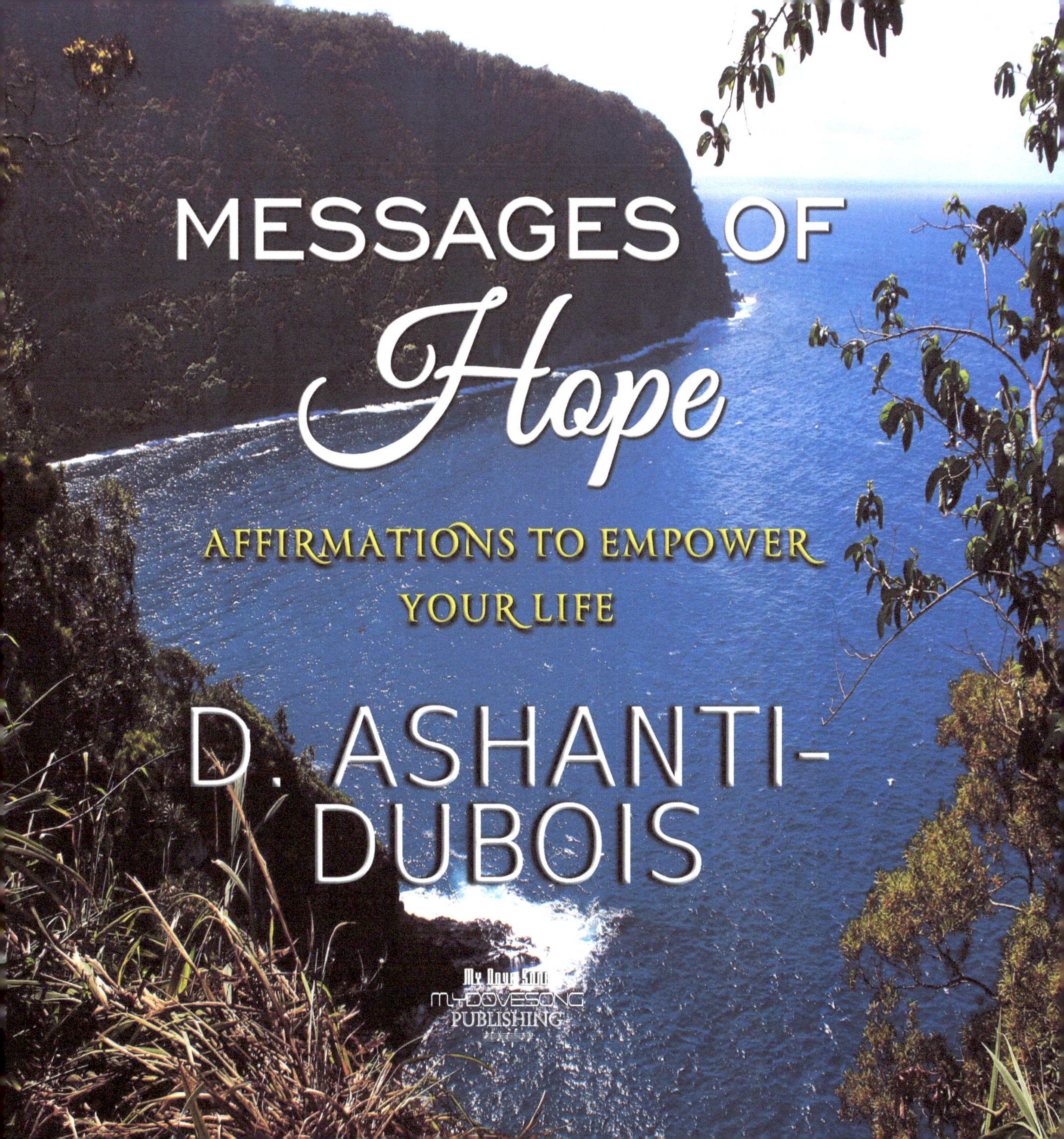
MESSAGES OF
Hope
AFFIRMATIONS TO EMPOWER
YOUR LIFE
D. ASHANTI-
DUBOIS
MYDOVESONG
PUBLISHING

Meditate on the love invocation below. Repeat three times a day for seven days.

My heart is open and I am ready to give and receive love. Love come to me...

I desire love, Love come to me. I desire hope, Hope come to me. I desire joy, Joy come to me.

I attract all things that bring me Love. I attract all things that bring me Hope. I attract all things that bring me Joy.

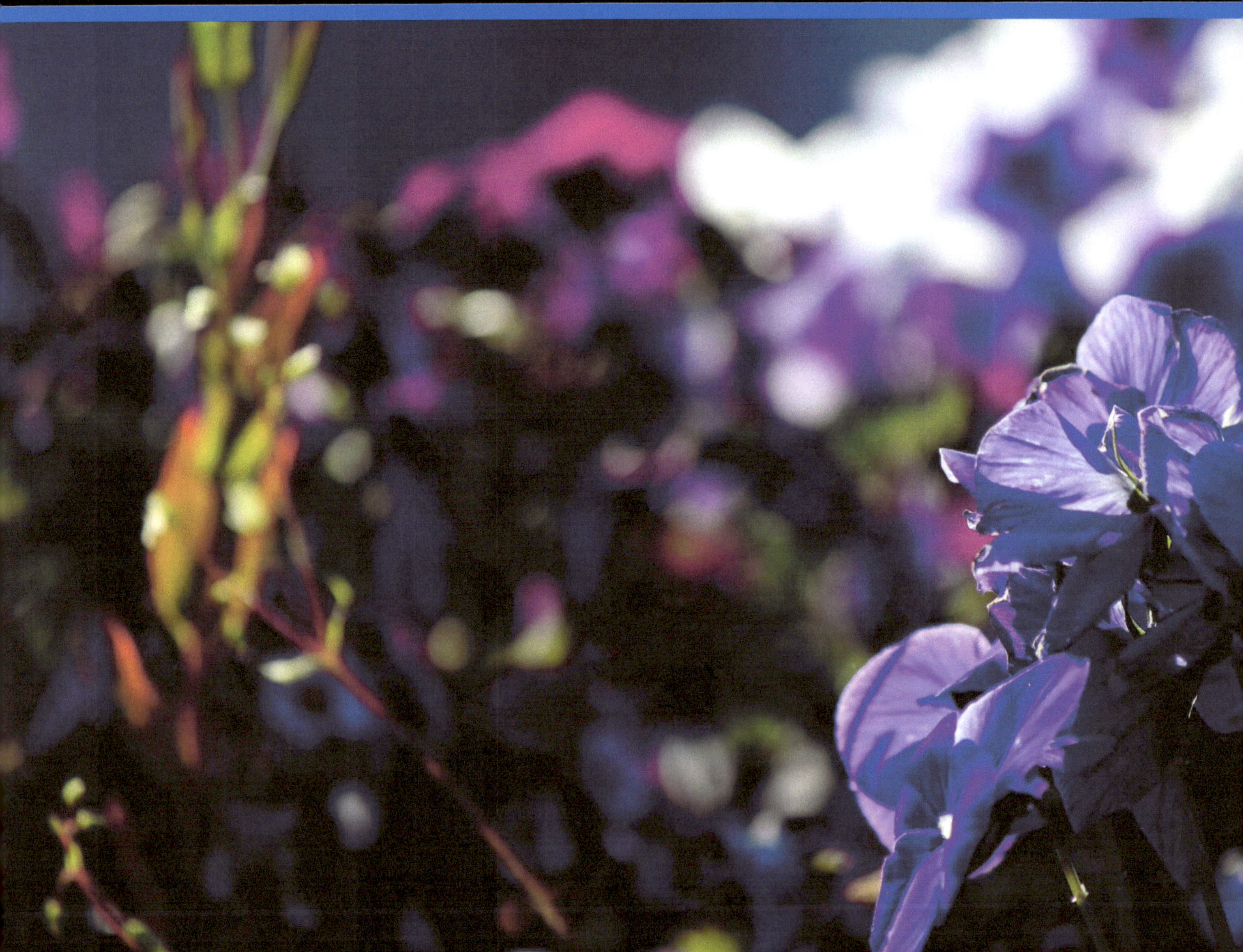

Divine Holy One, Come into my life so that I may live all that I wish to live and be all that I desire to be. Please take away all that stands between me and you and my hopes and dreams. Fulfill my daily needs, and empower me to be courageous, determined, loving, joyful, and prosperous. Manifest a miracle in me today.

In the name of the Holy One, Jesus Christ, I pray... Amen.

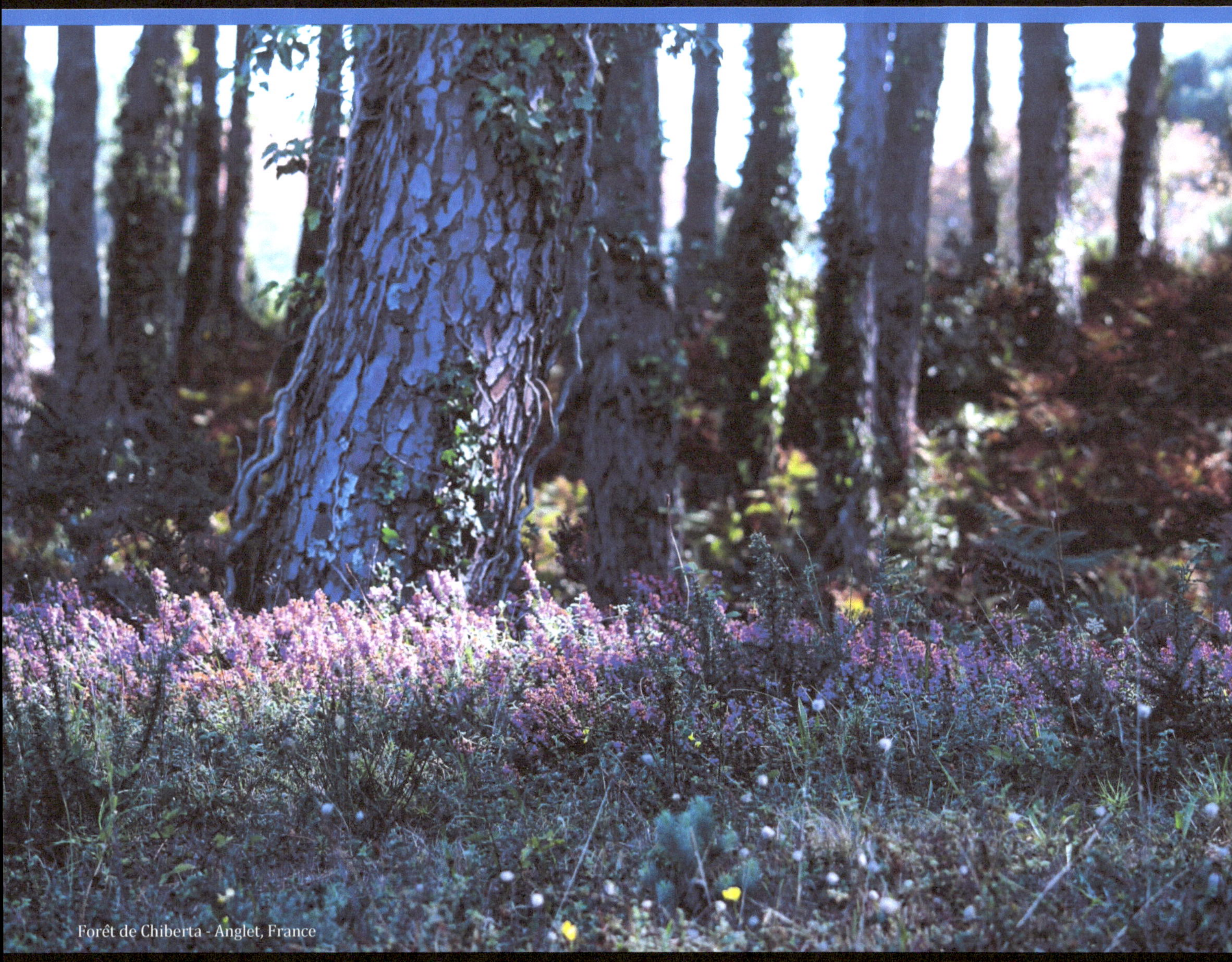

Forêt de Chiberta - Anglet, France

I am loved beyond measure because the Divine loves me.

I am protected. I am accepted. I am sheltered. I am blessed.

I am in the arms of the Divine.

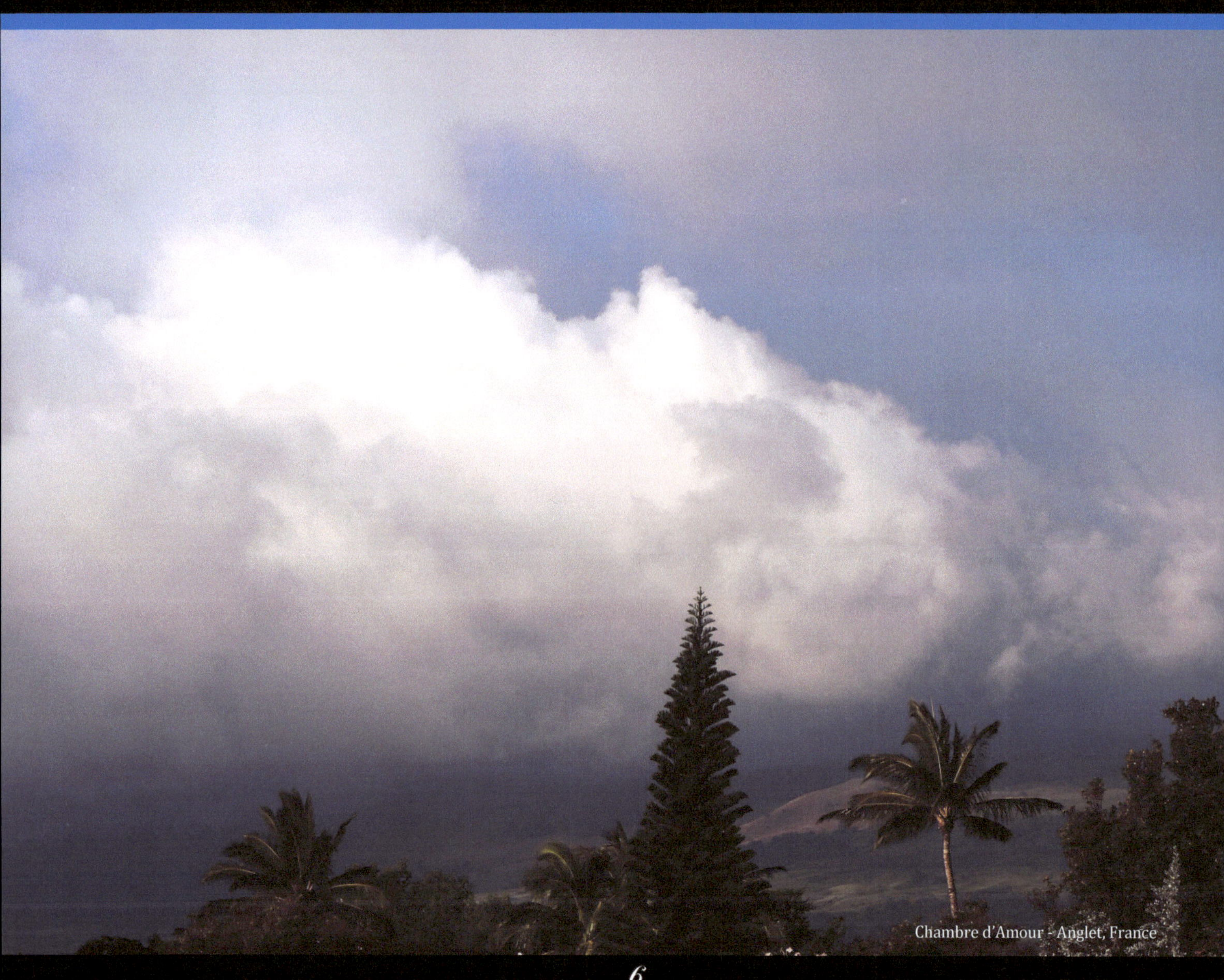

Chambre d'Amour - Anglet, France

My life is a true miracle in the making.

Every challenge, crisis, and hardship I face, makes me stronger in my heart, my spirit, and mind.

I am courageous, I am victorious, and I shall stand.

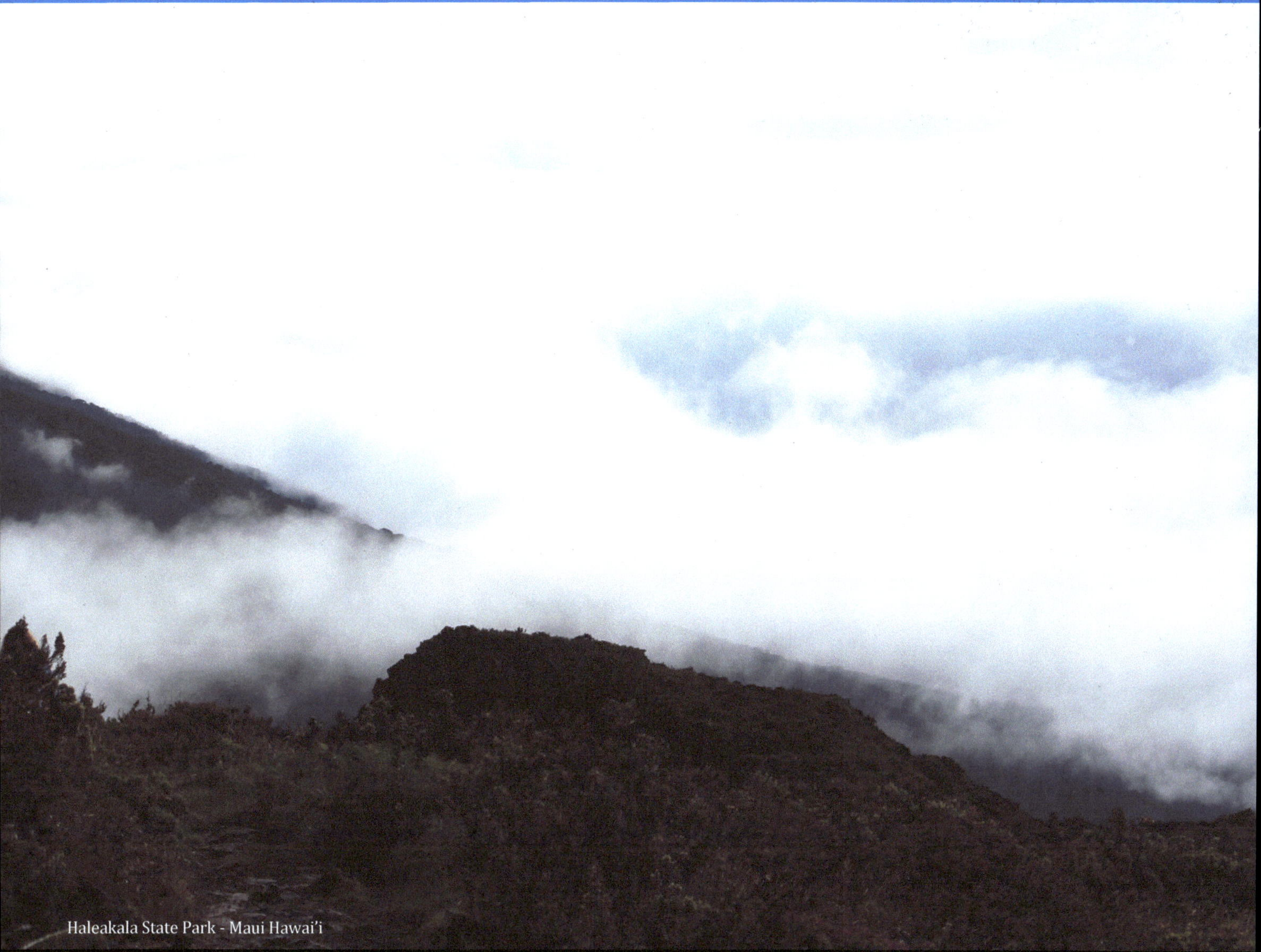

Haleakala State Park - Maui Hawai'i

Today is the day I fulfill my dreams and I will not cease until it is done.
I will accomplish something today.

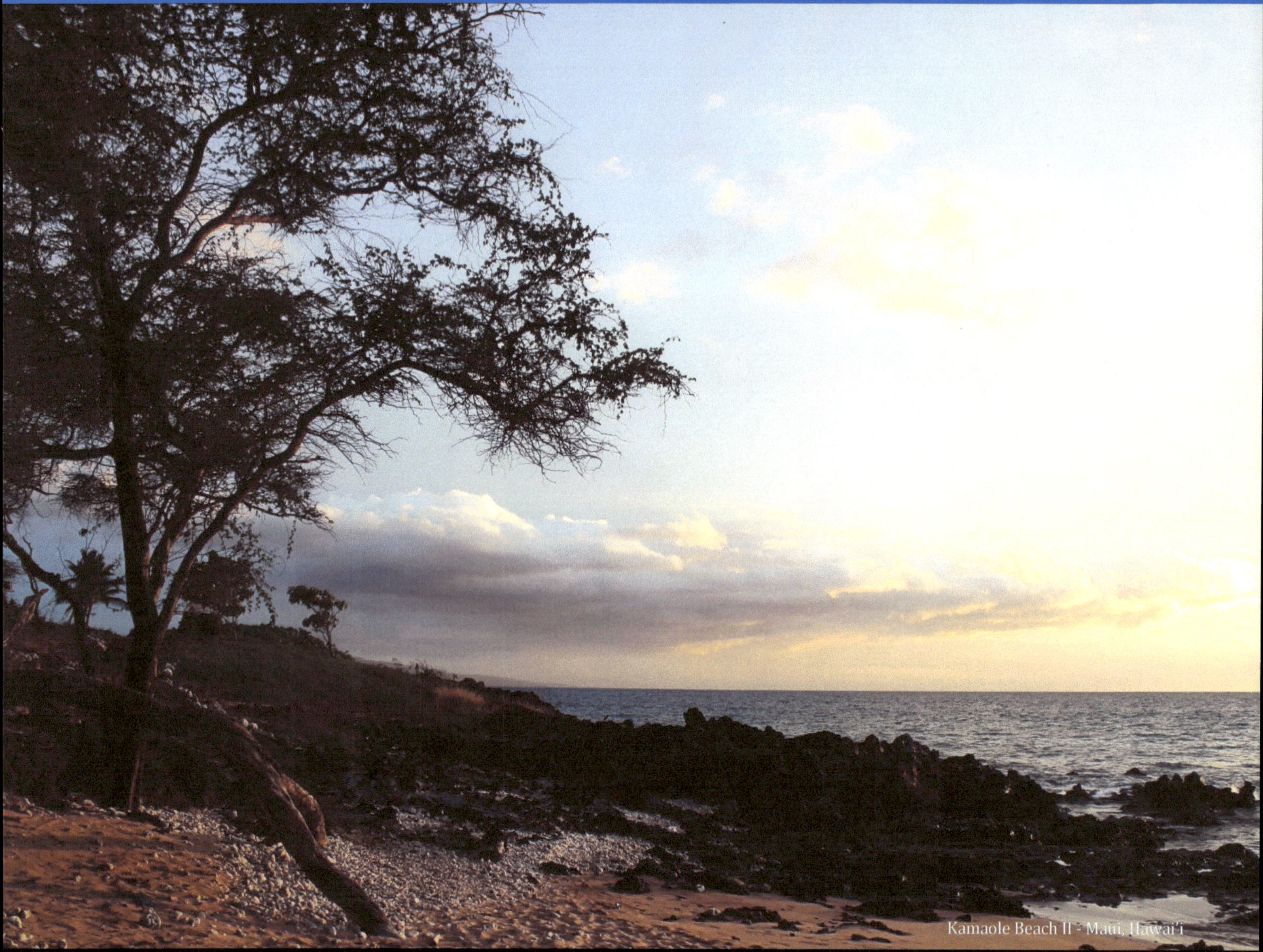

Kamaole Beach II - Maui, Hawai'i

I am not afraid.

I am courageously walking my path with faith.

I shall fear no evil.

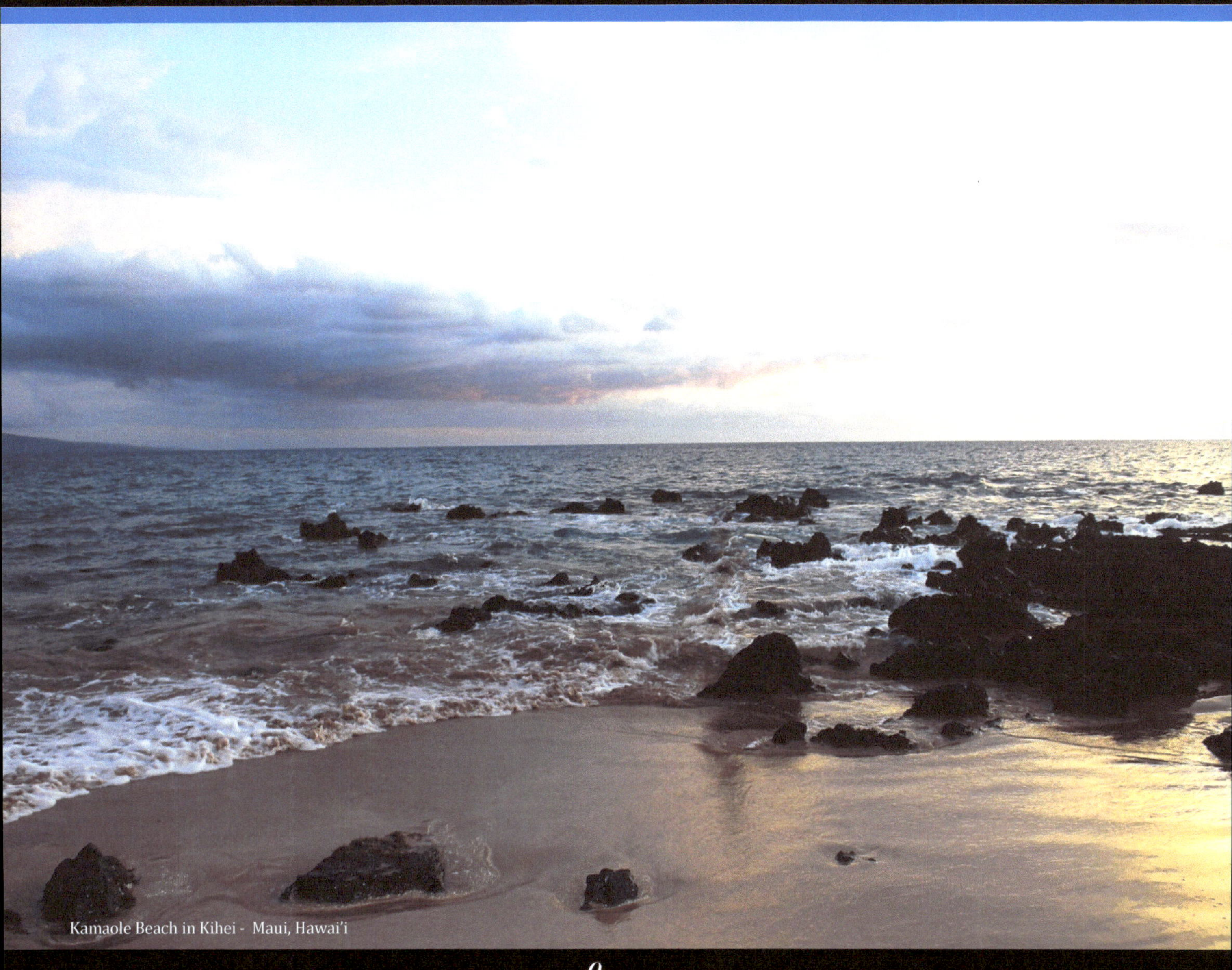

Kamaole Beach in Kihei - Maui, Hawai'i

I already have everything I need to be happy.

Love lies within me. I am complete.

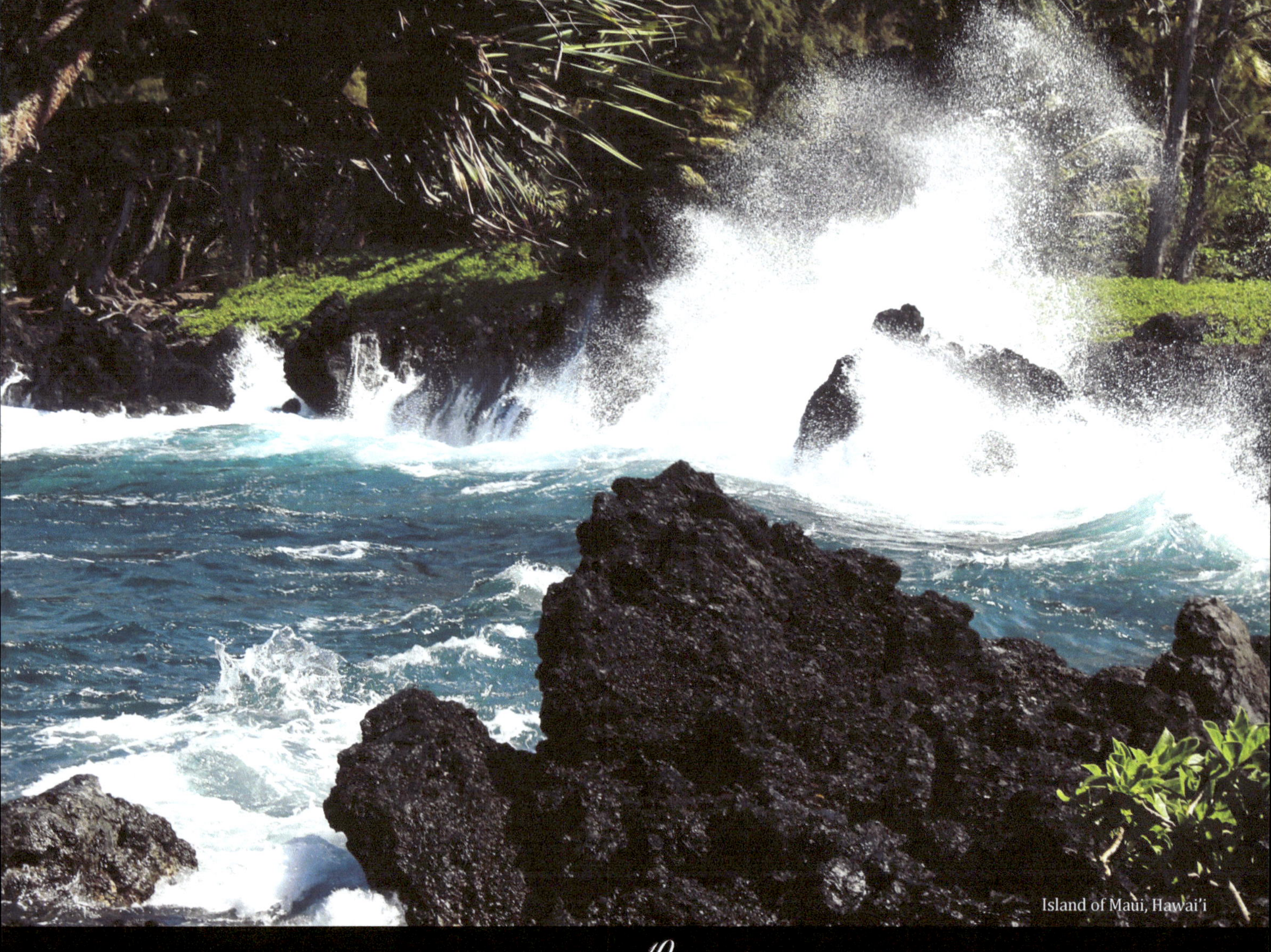

Island of Maui, Hawai'i

I have the power within me to manifest my dreams and change my life.

I see it. I feel it. I believe it. It is possible. It is done.

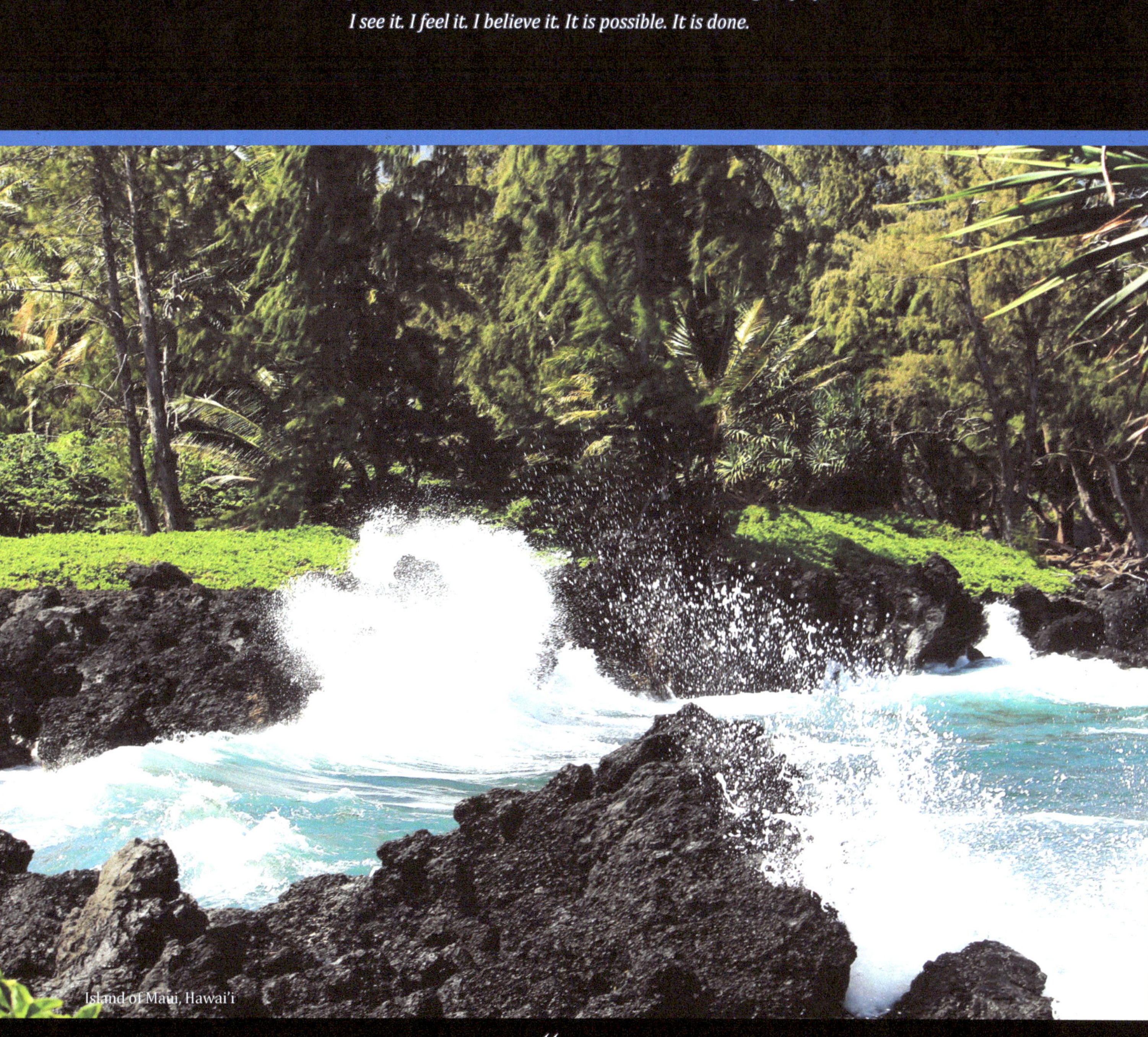

Island of Maui, Hawai'i

I am free from my past and I choose to live without guilt, regret, or pain.

I will not go back, but shall move forward.

And I leave all of yesterday in the hands of the Divine.

I stand on the promises of GOD.

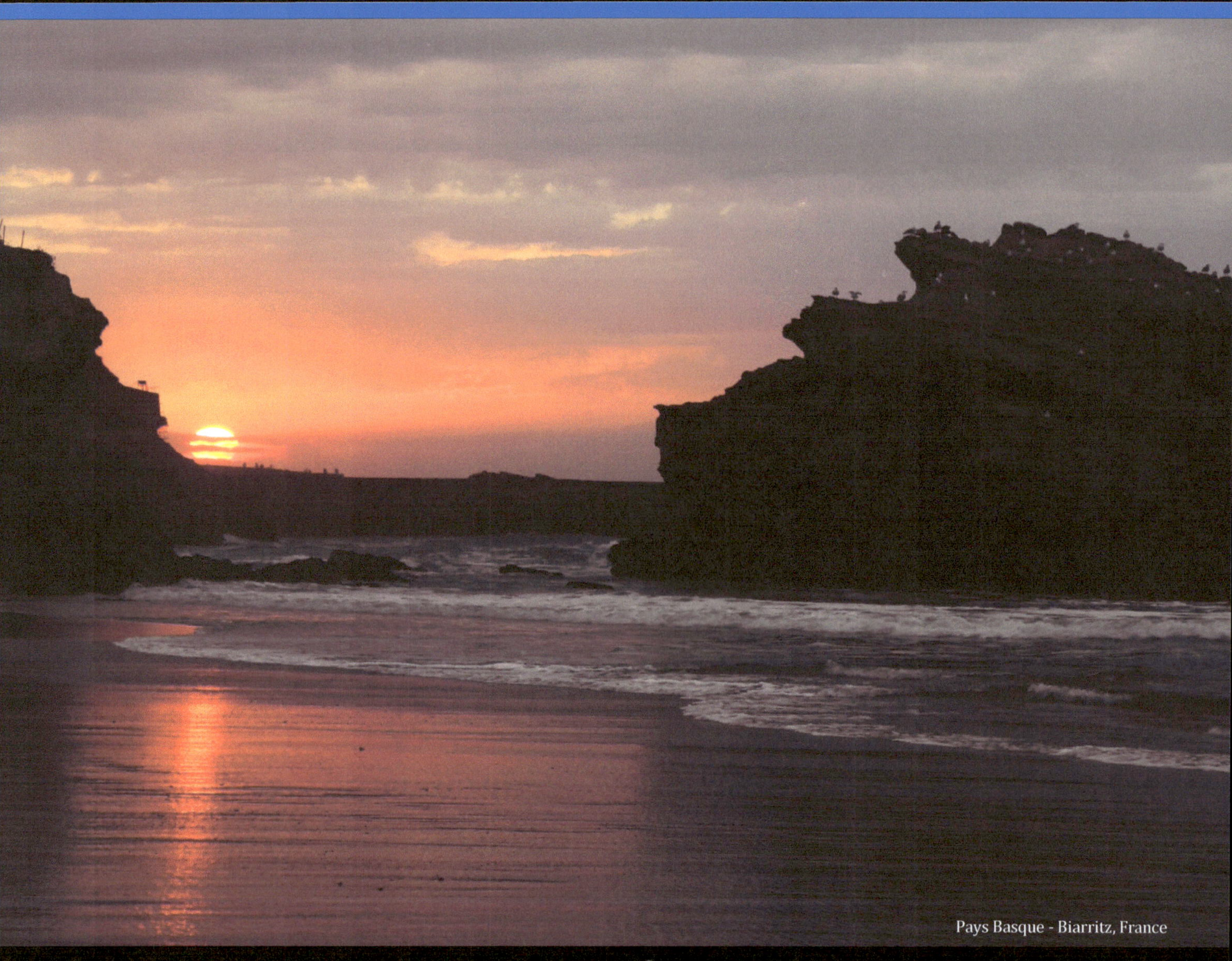

Pays Basque - Biarritz, France

All the good I desire will come to me.

And by faith, I will do all that is necessary to achieve my goals.

My faith is the promise of great things to come.

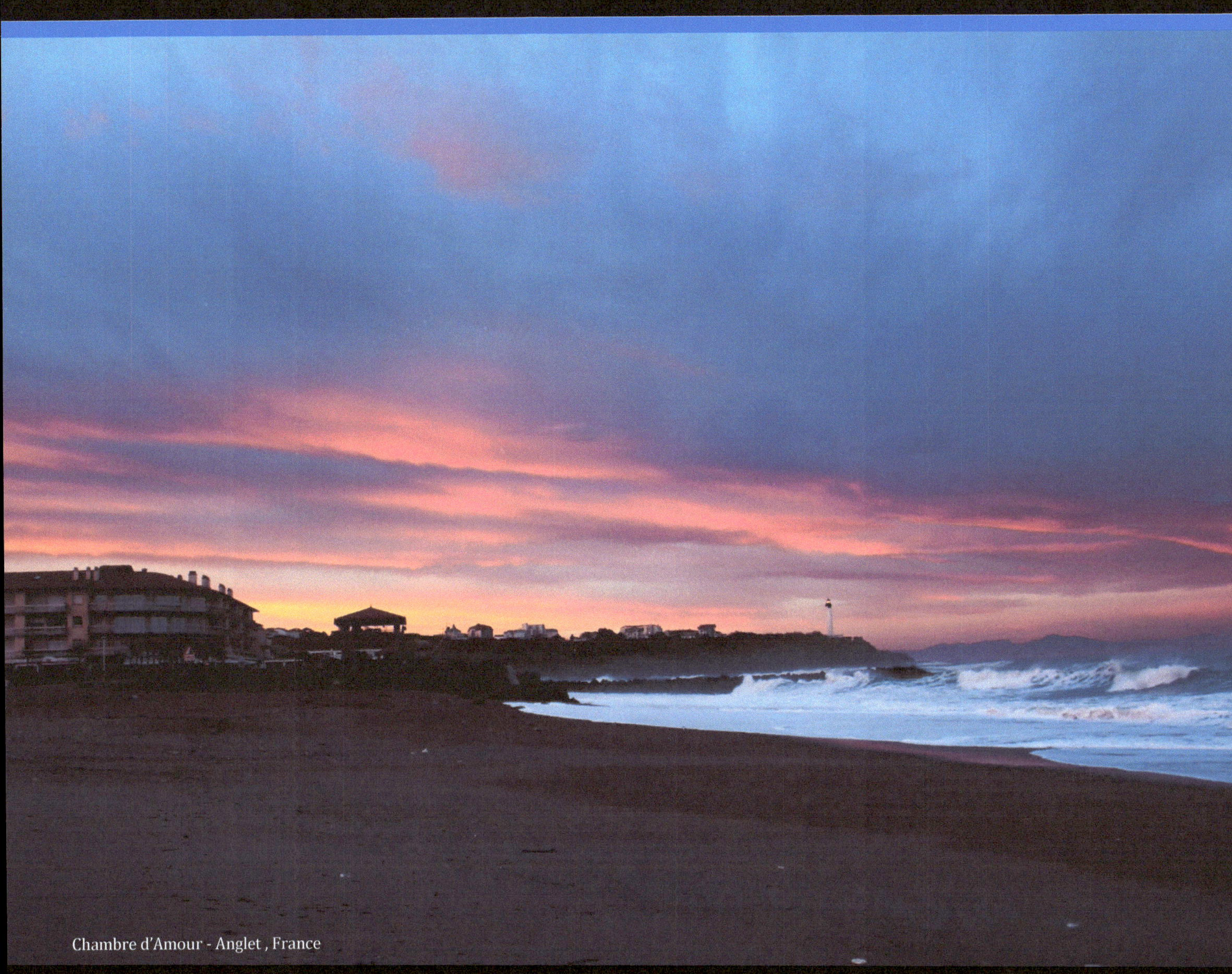

Chambre d'Amour - Anglet , France

I let go of the pain of yesterday, I have no fear of tomorrow.
Today is a day of new beginnings. I expect great things.

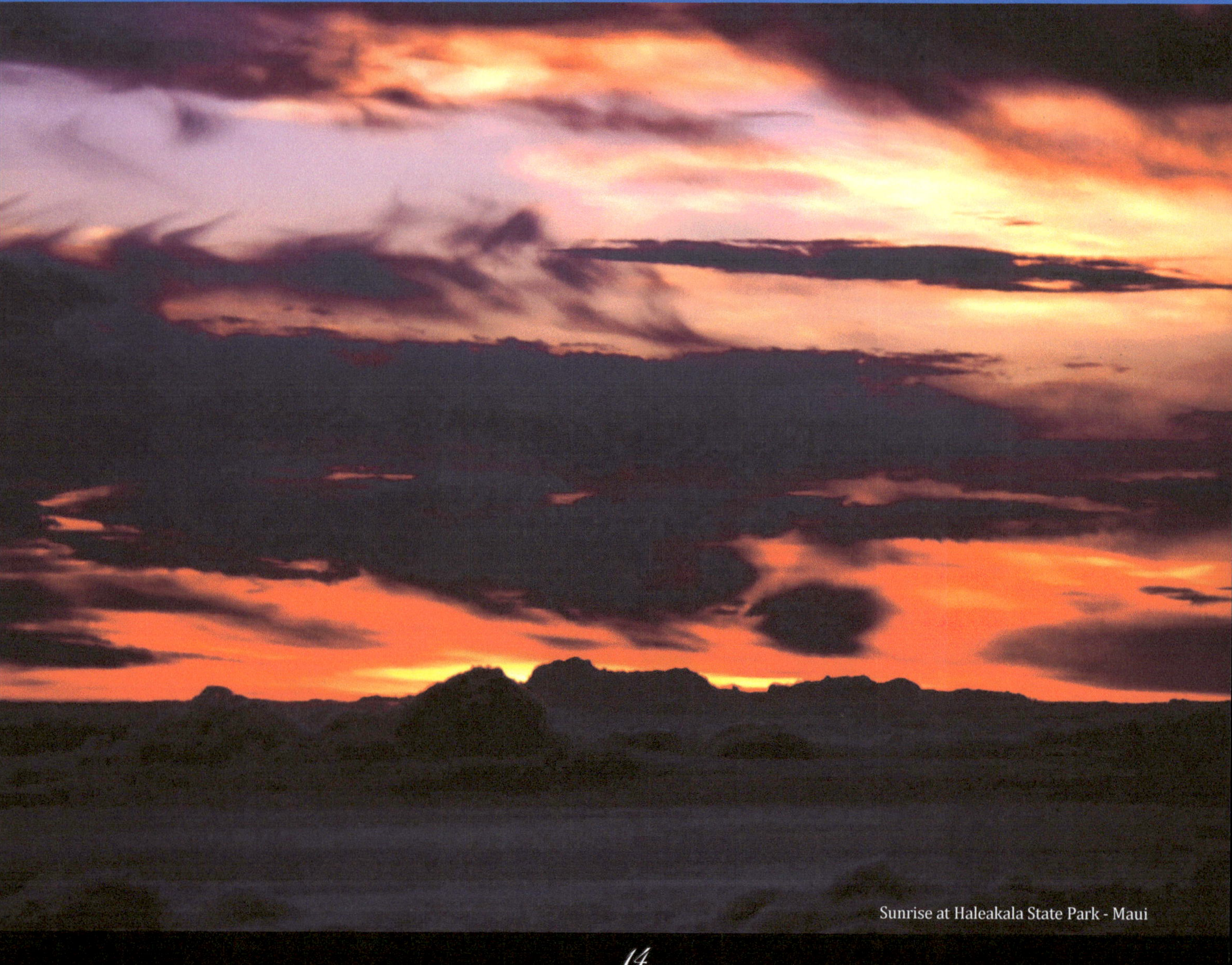
Sunrise at Haleakala State Park - Maui

I love me enough to accept my shortcomings as well as my greatest attributes.
I am truly a worthy human being and I am worthy of all good things,
not because I am perfect, but because I am loved by the Holy Divine.

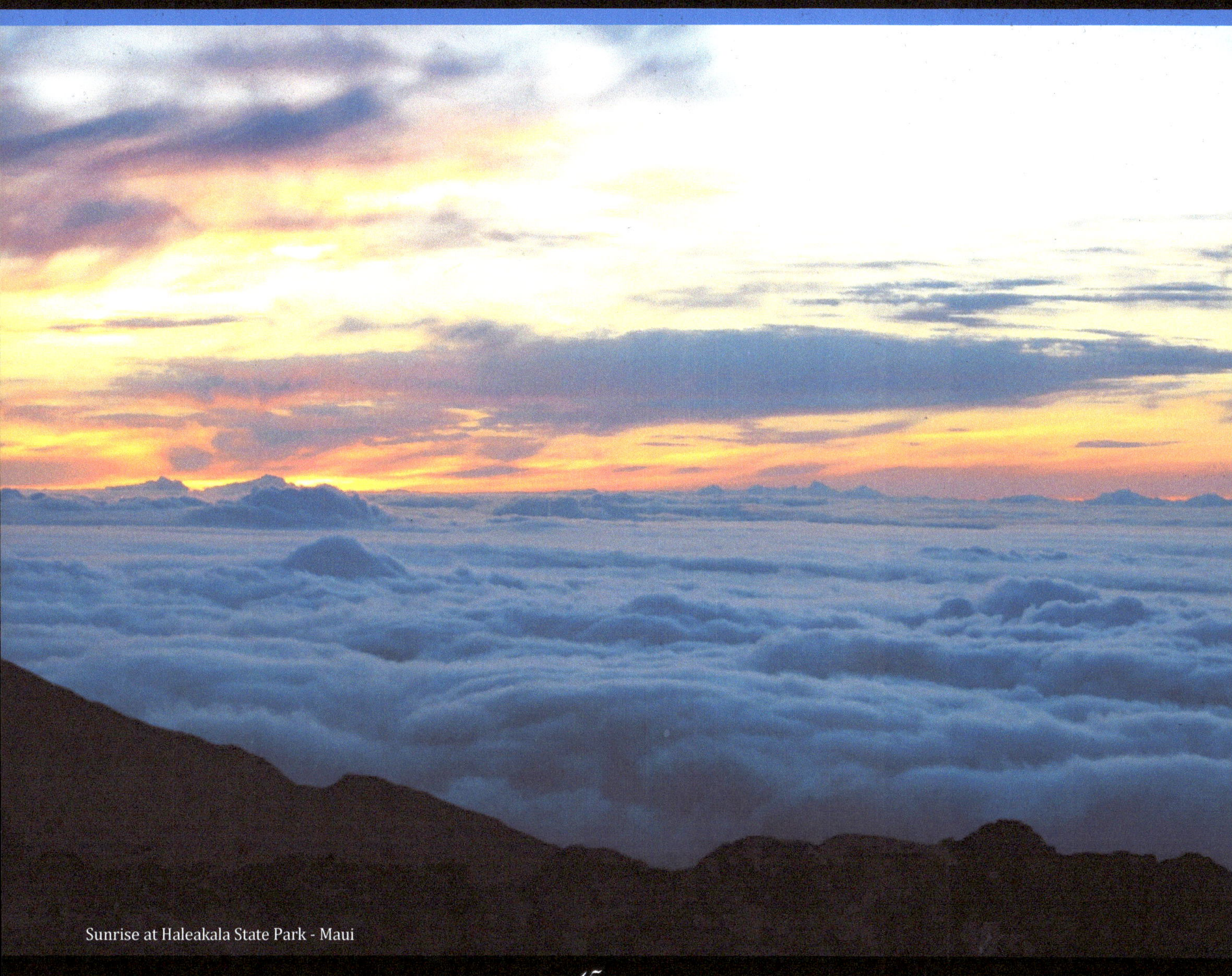

Sunrise at Haleakala State Park - Maui

I choose to let go of all things that hurt me. I do not fear change.

I do no worry for the future. I am not sorry for the past.

I did not give up; I let go of these things.

I claim victory over everything

that prevents me from having a happy life.

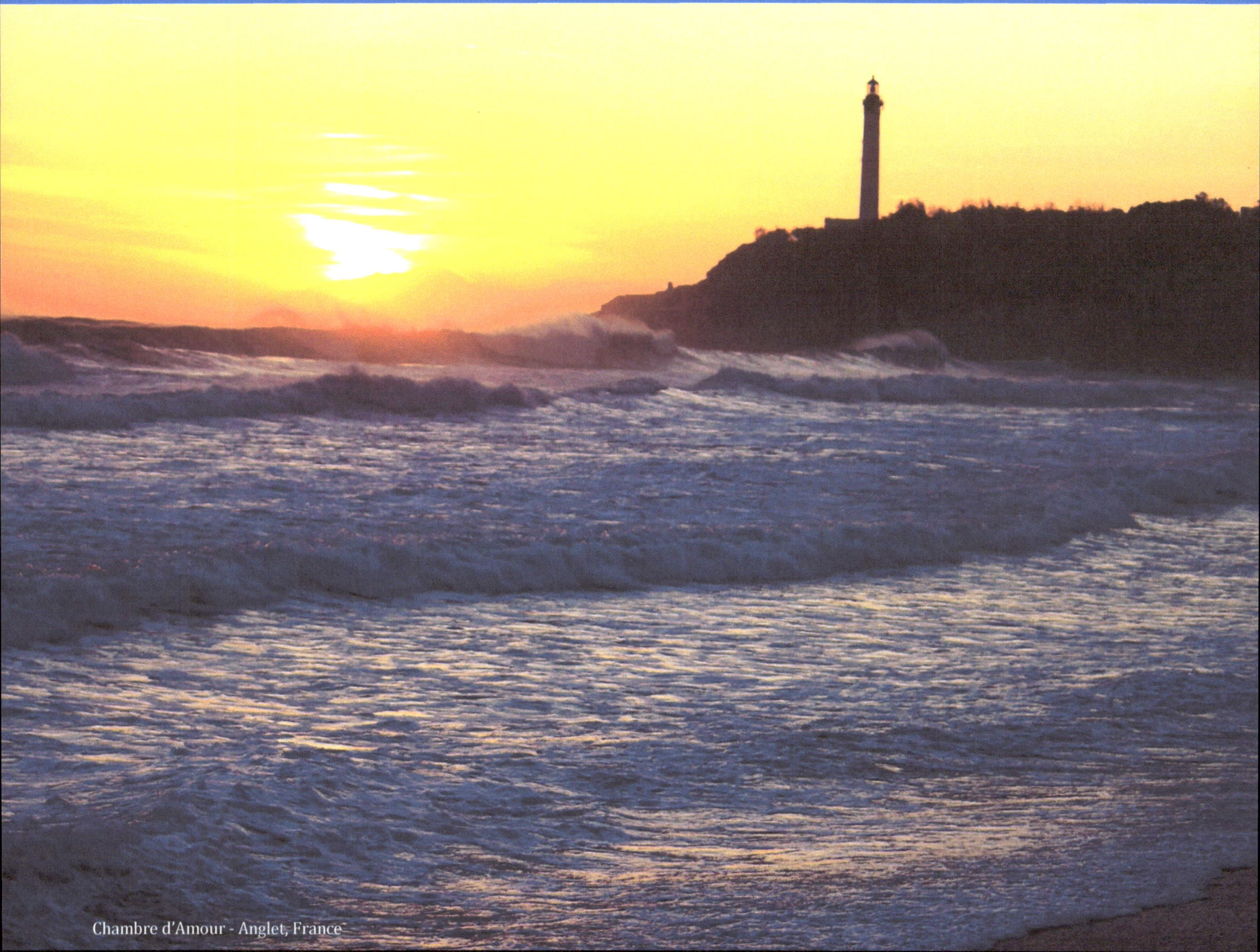

Chambre d'Amour - Anglet, France

I attract all things I need to my life and release all I do not.

Morning Sky Cinq Cantons - Anglet, France

I put my mind on things that give me strength and the hopes that comfort me.

The past can no longer hurt me because I do not live there anymore.

I have moved on to my new home, and it is a place of peace.

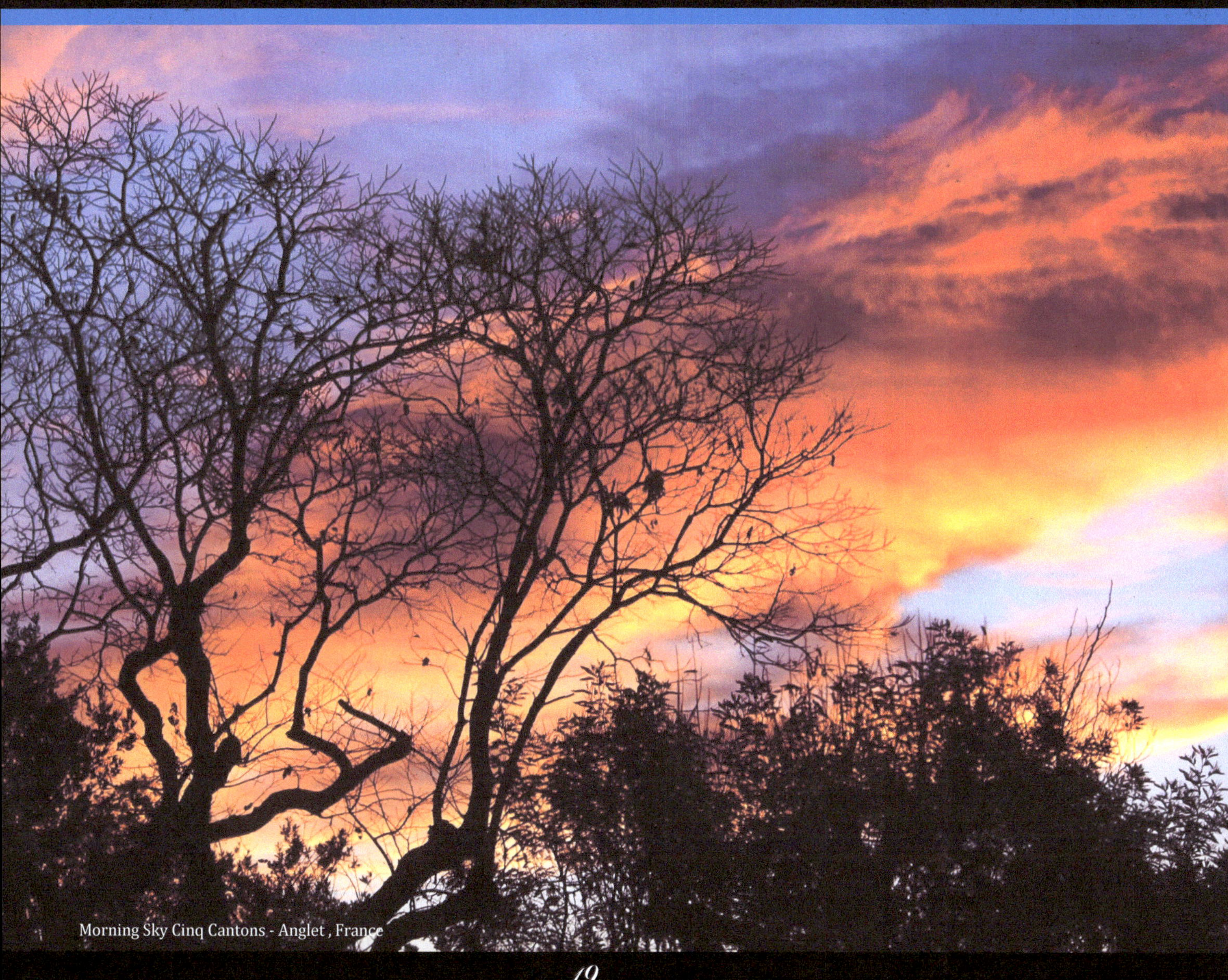

Morning Sky Cinq Cantons - Anglet , France

I invest in my possibility.

All I need to be already exists within me.

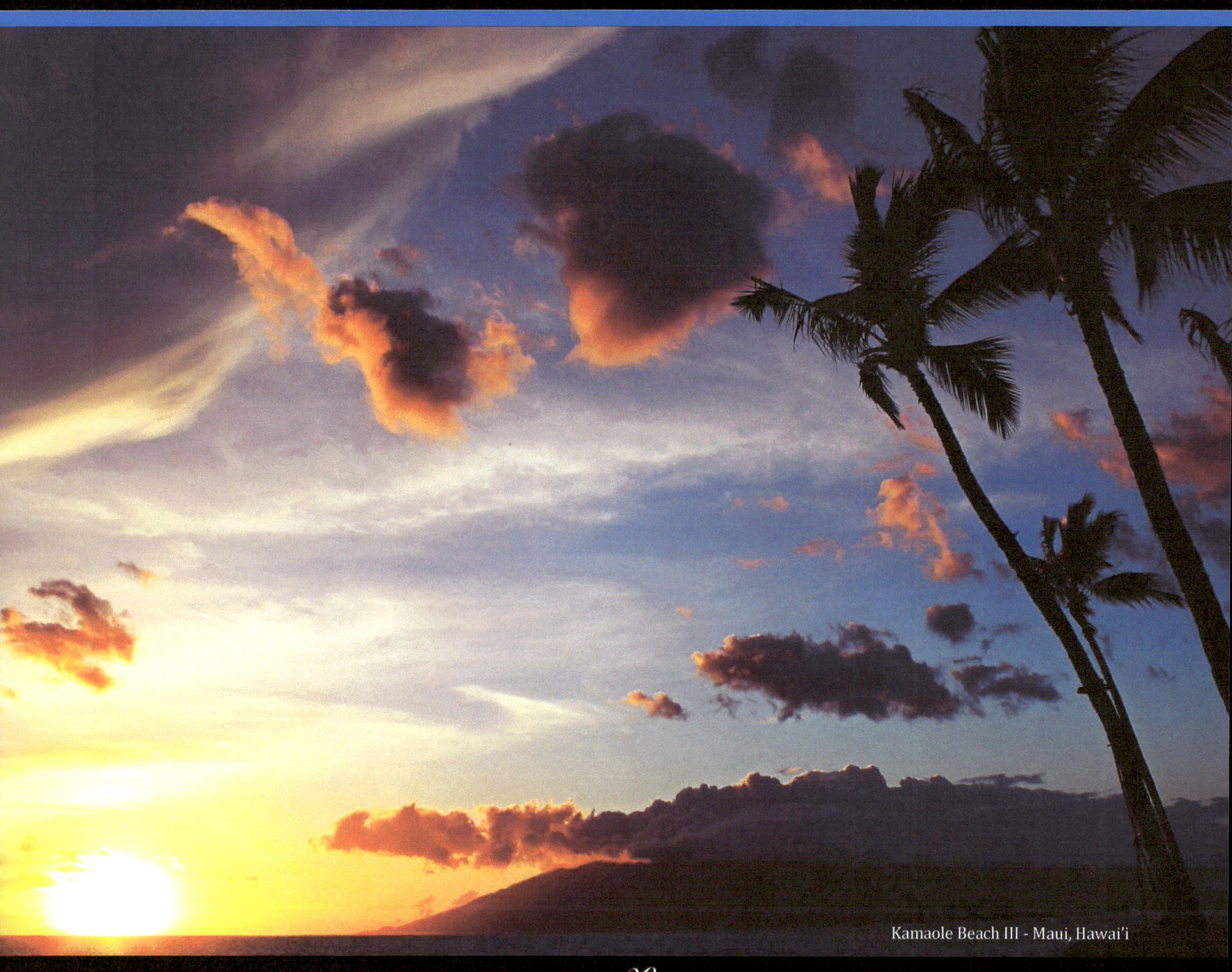

Kamaole Beach III - Maui, Hawai'i

I put in my hope in the Divine GOD,

and I am healed.

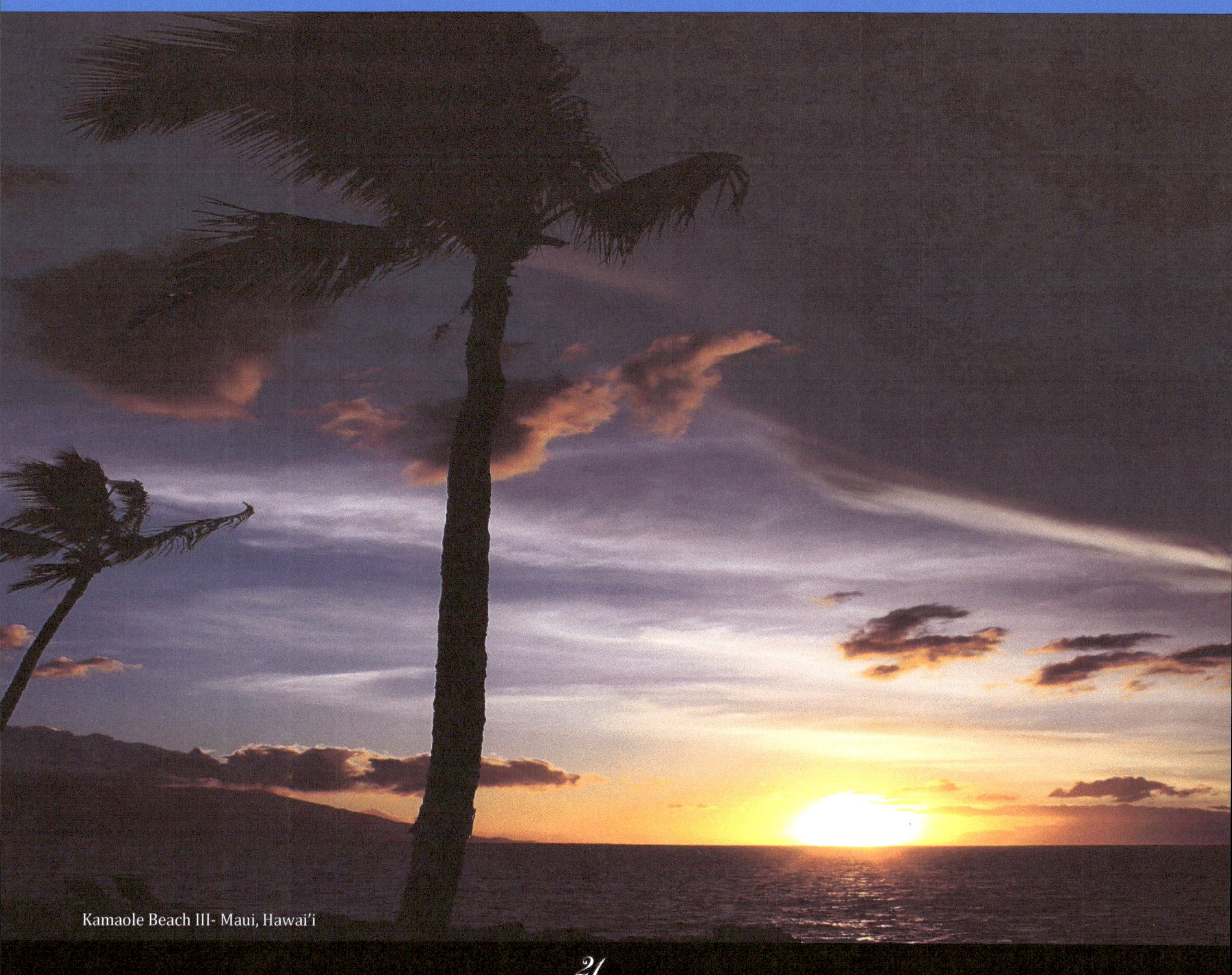

Kamaole Beach III- Maui, Hawai'i

I will endure the shifts of the seasons and tremors of the land. I am deeply rooted in Divine wisdom, power, and love.

I will not be made to fall down in the face of adversity. I am strong, courageous, and believing.

I shall not be moved.

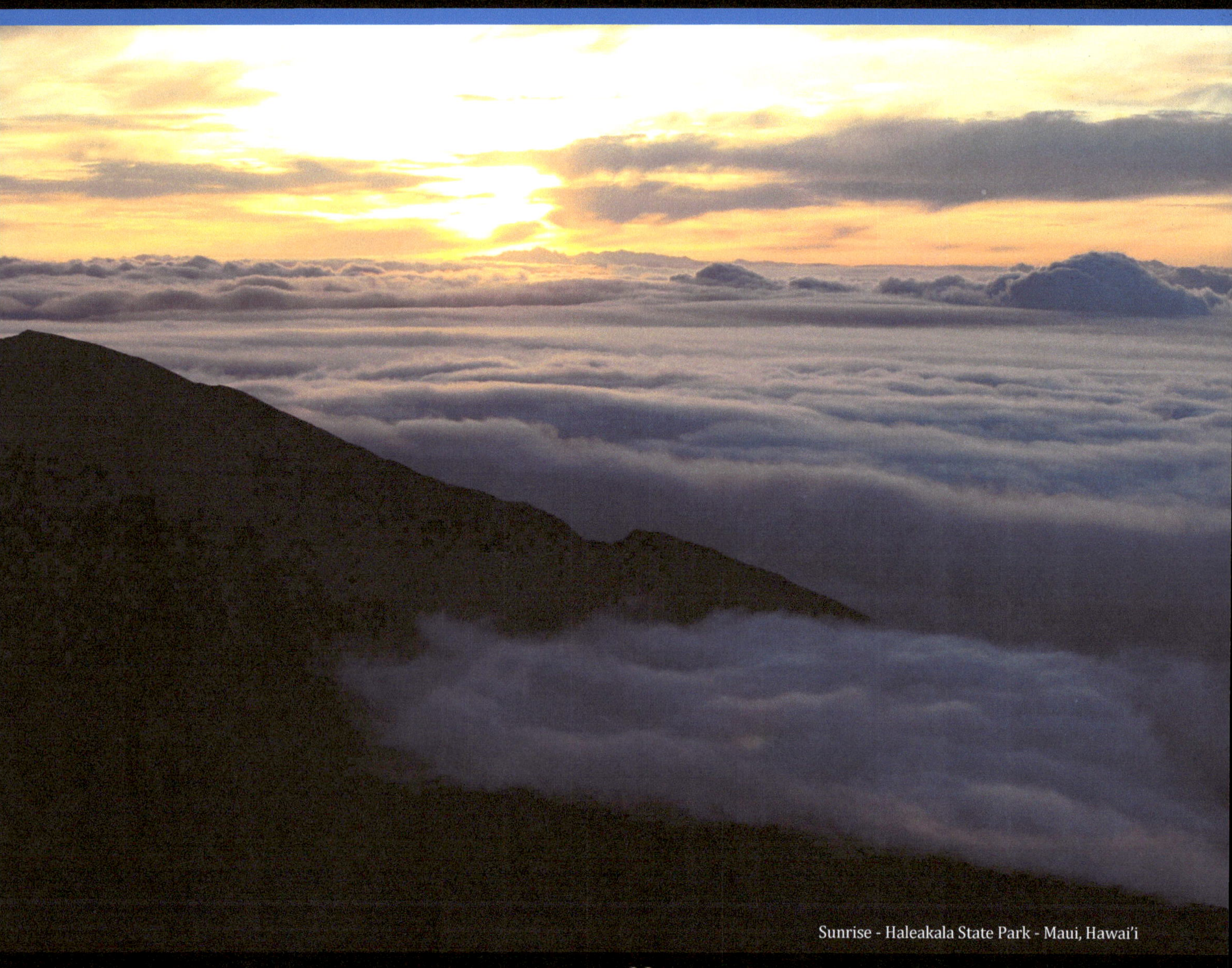

Sunrise - Haleakala State Park - Maui, Hawai'i

For every road that I've traveled, I have learned along the way. For every path that was mistaken, I will not walk that way again. Every error has been forgiven and every lesson I have learned. I am wiser for the journey and I am strong and I am moving on.

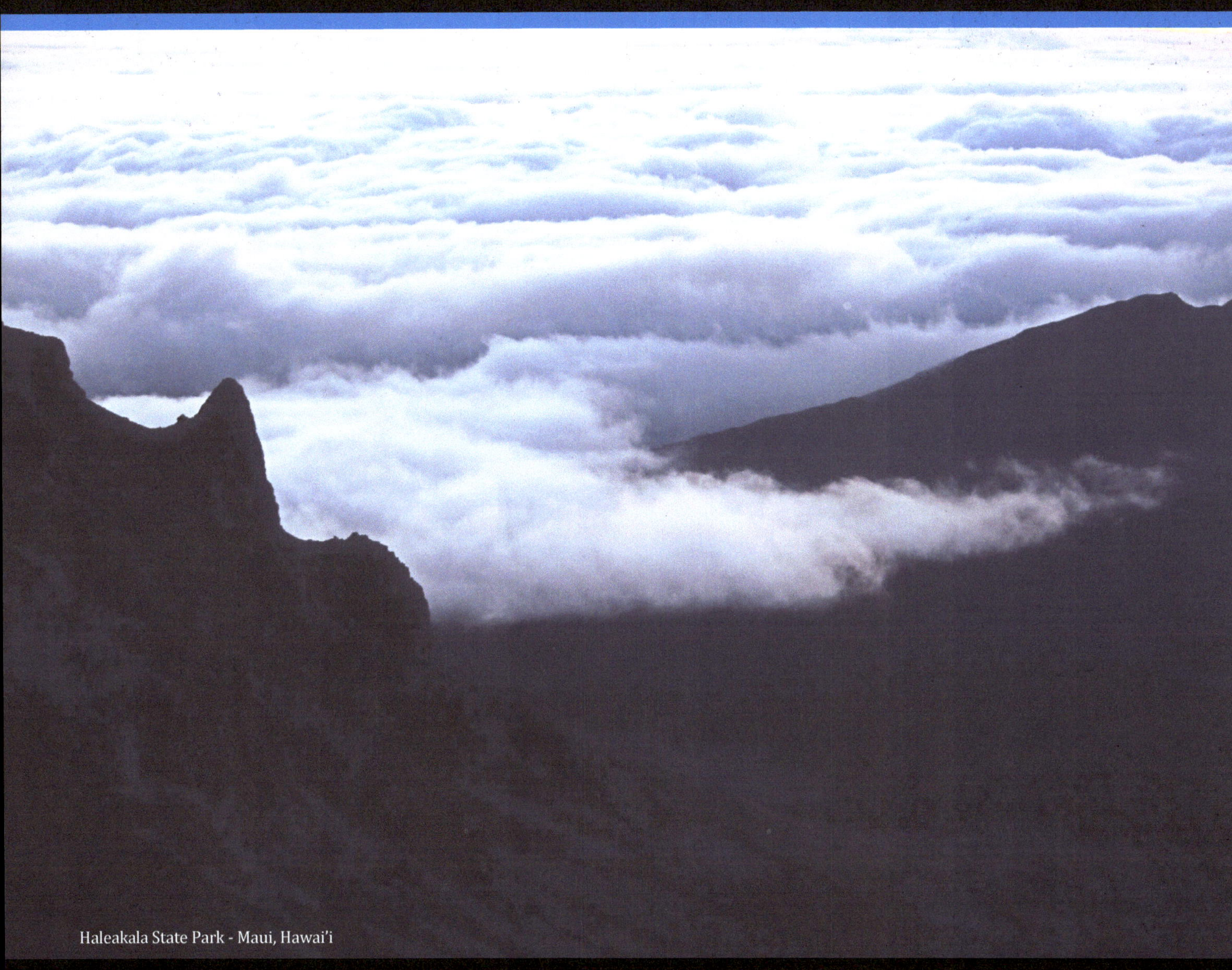

Haleakala State Park - Maui, Hawai'i

I am no one's victim. I take full responsibility for my life and I rise to the occasion to rebuild it if necessary.
I may bend, but I will not break. I will hold on to my faith and will endure.
I am like a tree deeply rooted in faith. I am strong, and I am not afraid.

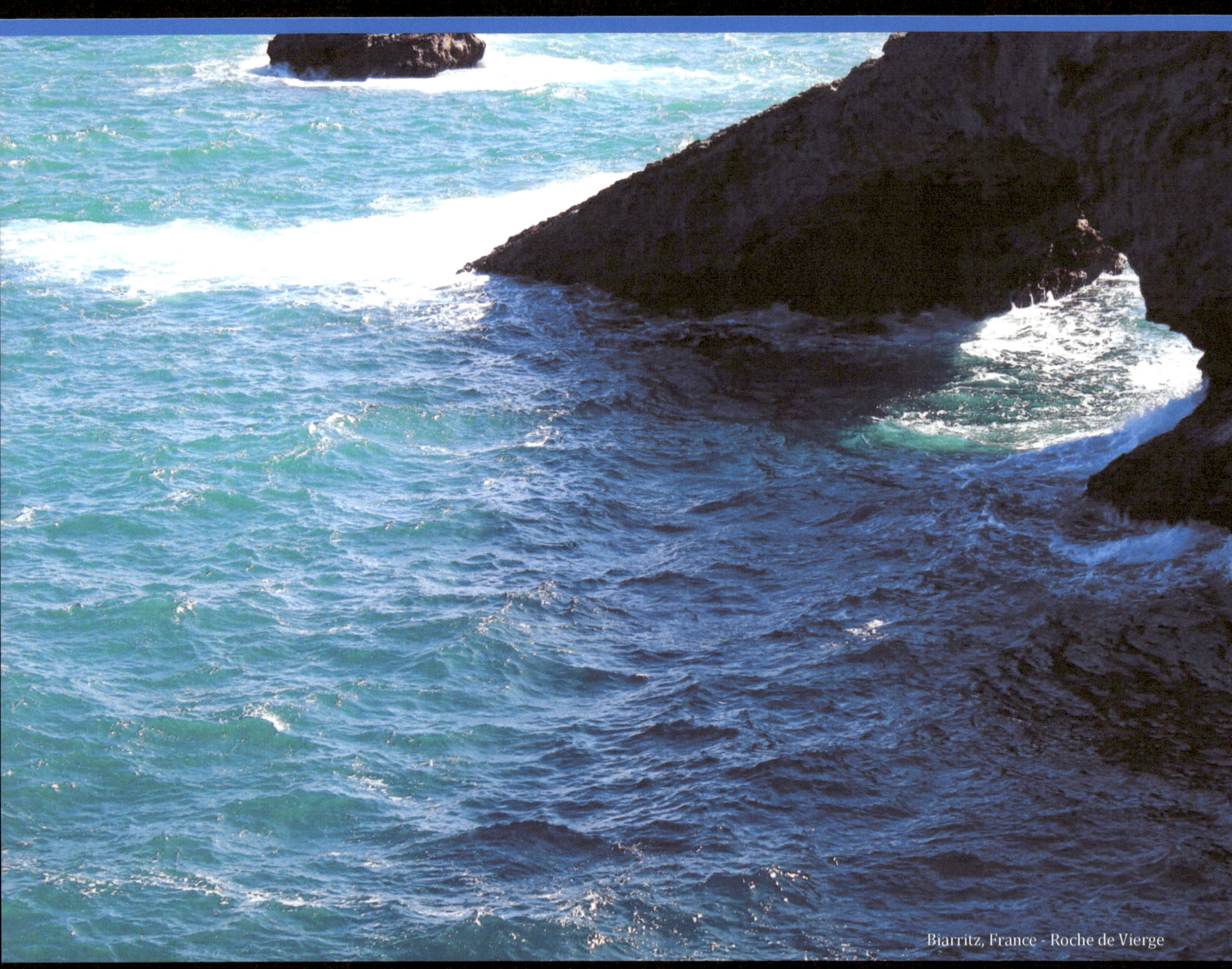

Biarritz, France - Roche de Vierge

I will grow and flourish into the happiest person I can possibly be. I will live my life in the fullest possible way. I will triumph over every difficult situation with courage, faith, humility, hope, and love.

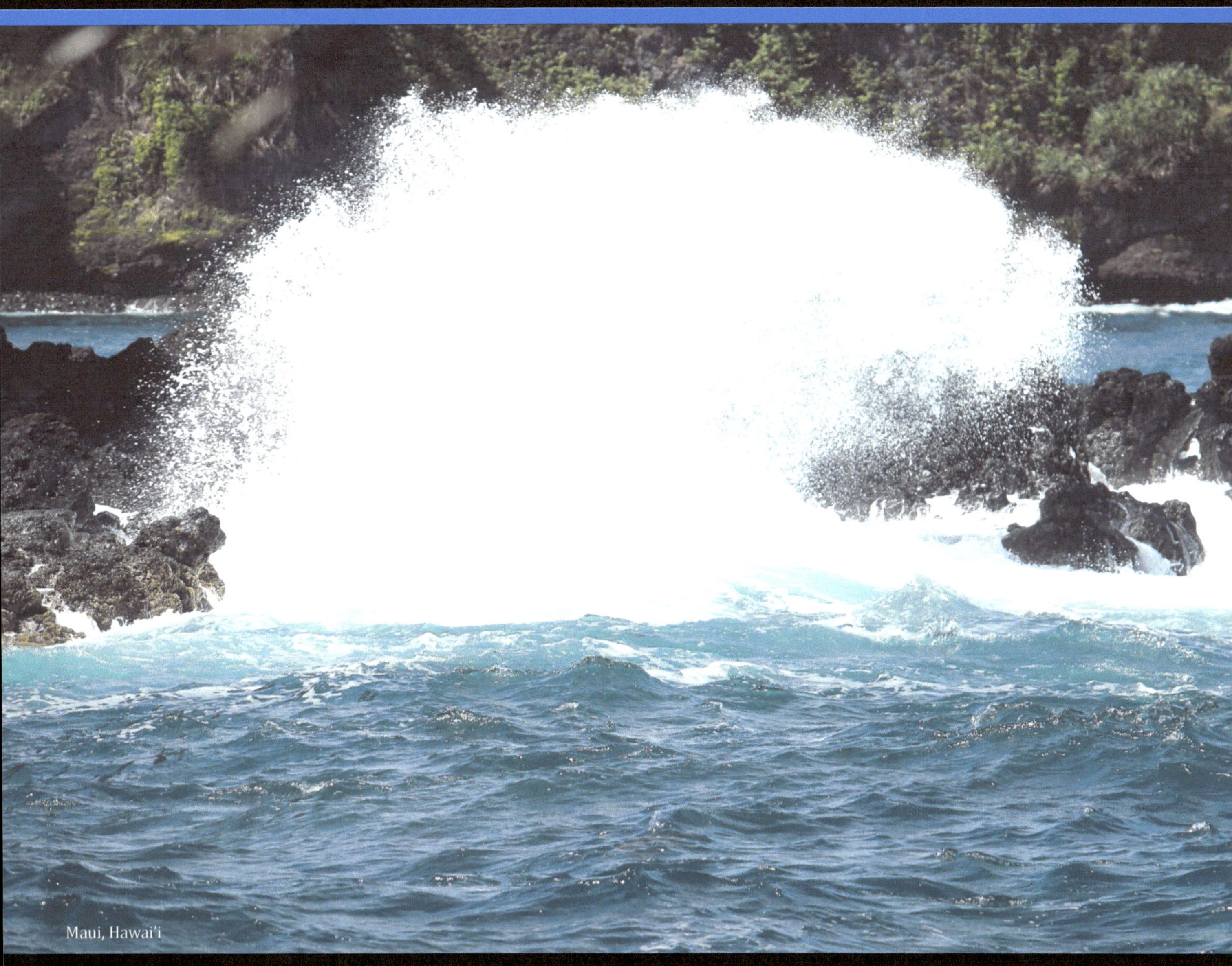

Maui, Hawai'i

I am made from love. And true love surrounds me in every way.

I am never without love, because love dwells within me.

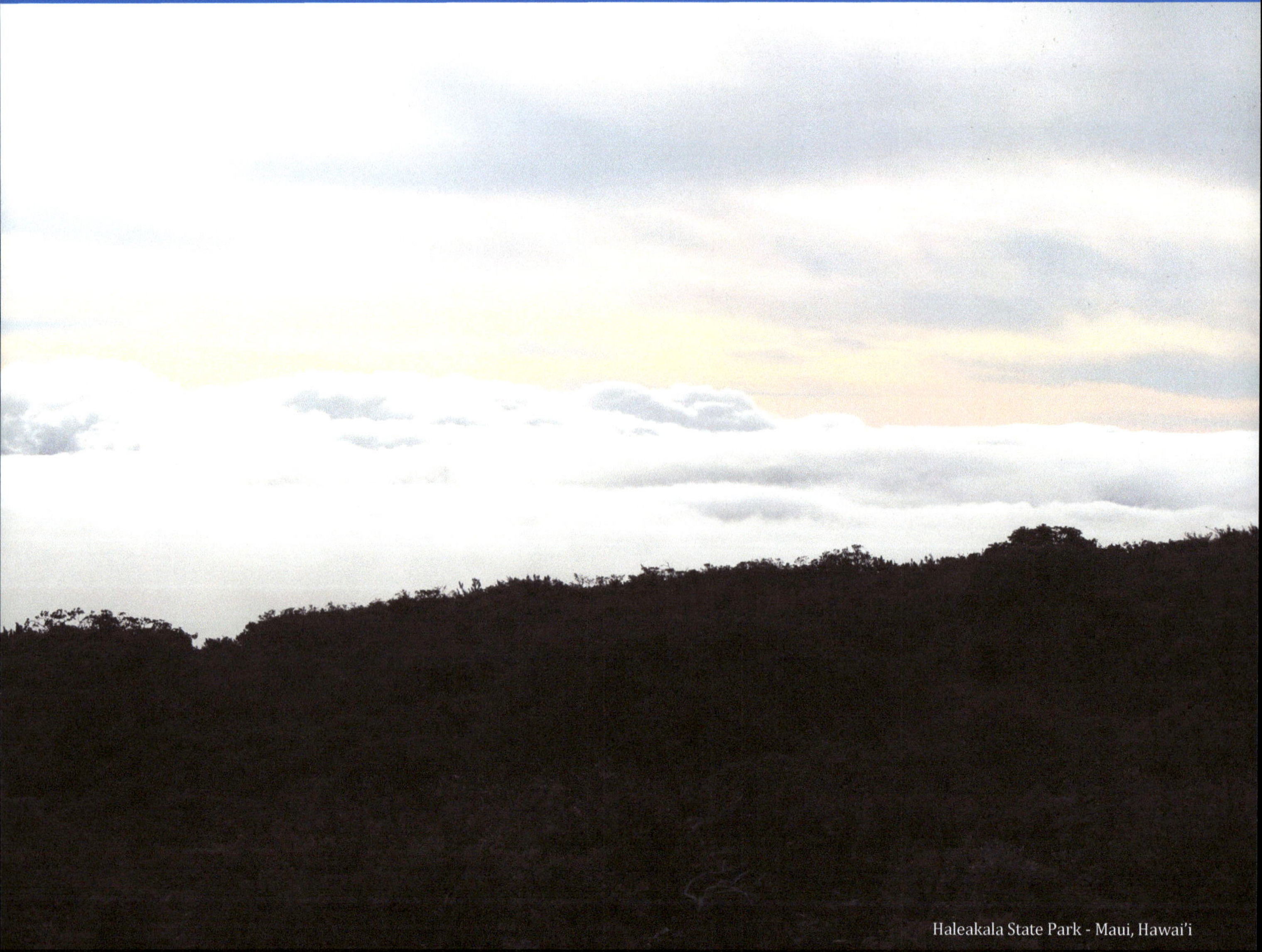

Haleakala State Park - Maui, Hawai'i

I have hope and hope has me.
I am holding on to what keeps me strong.
And even if I grow weary, I know that my problems will be overcome.

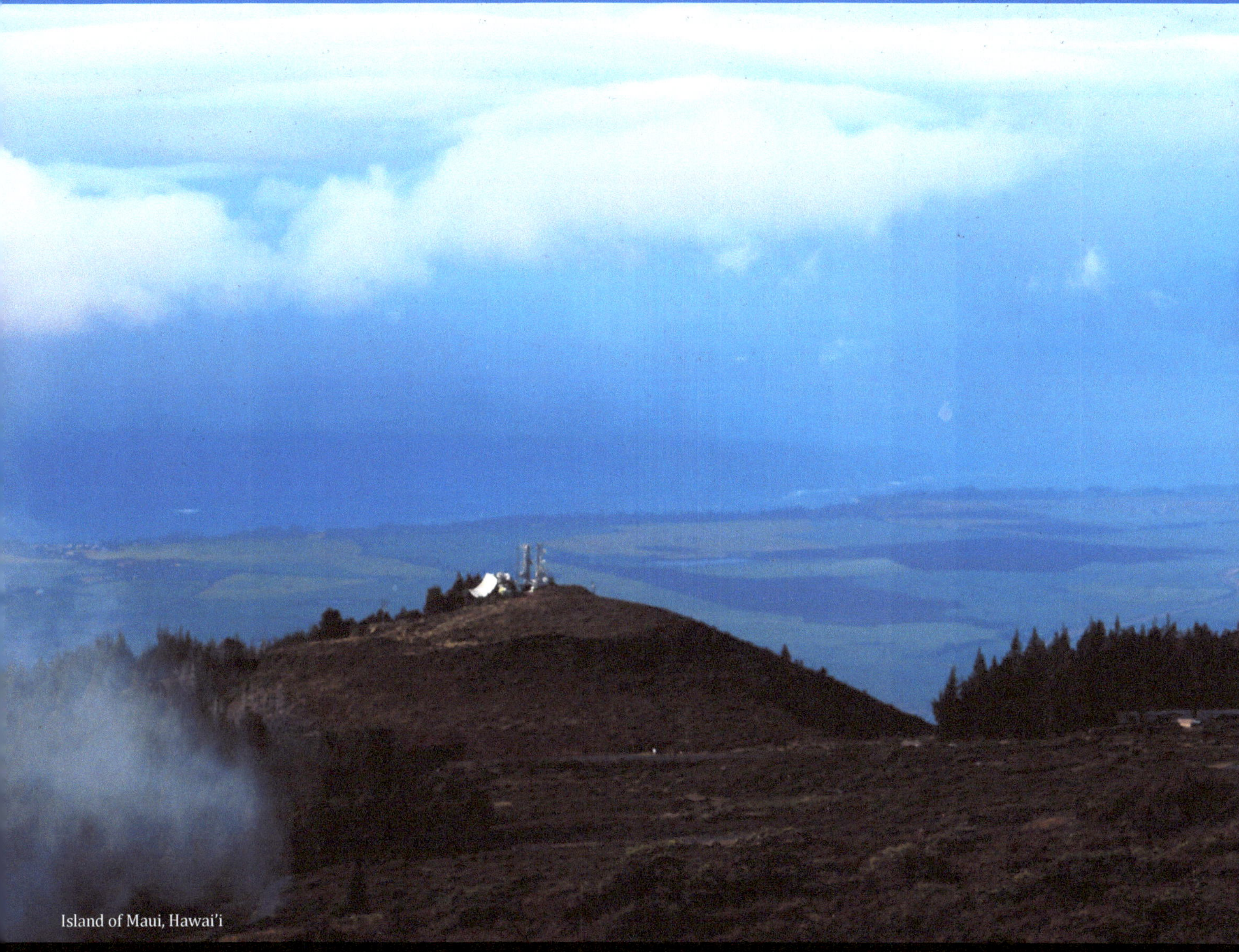

Island of Maui, Hawai'i

Repeat each affirmation at least three times to counter negative thoughts and fears. Think three positive thoughts for every negative that enters your mind. (Example: I am not afraid. I am courageous. I will overcome this.)

When you repeat an affirmation seven times, the message becomes your inner-voice.

The key to manifesting your desire is to expect miracles. I Am Beautiful I Am Healed

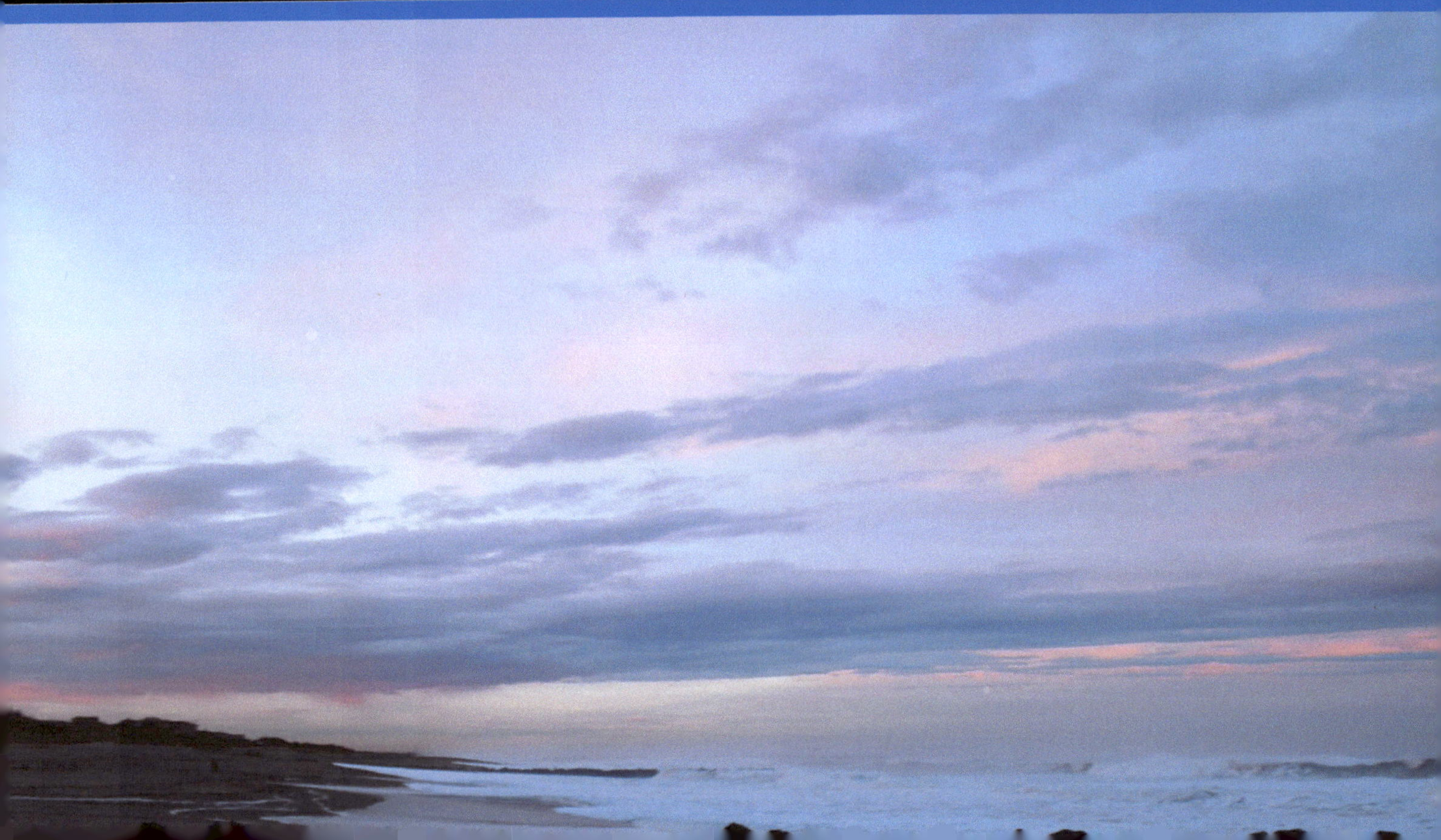

I Am Prosperous. I Am Wise. I Am Faithful. I Am Courageous. I Am Strong. I Am Confident. I am Intelligent.
I am Fearless. I am Positive. I am Determined. I am Capable. I am Generous. I am Giving. I am Trustworthy.
I am Patient. I am Decisive. I am Talented. I Am Secure. I Am Kind. I Am Loving. I am Happy.
I am Powerful. I am Complete. I am Focused. I am Free. I am Loved. I am Me.

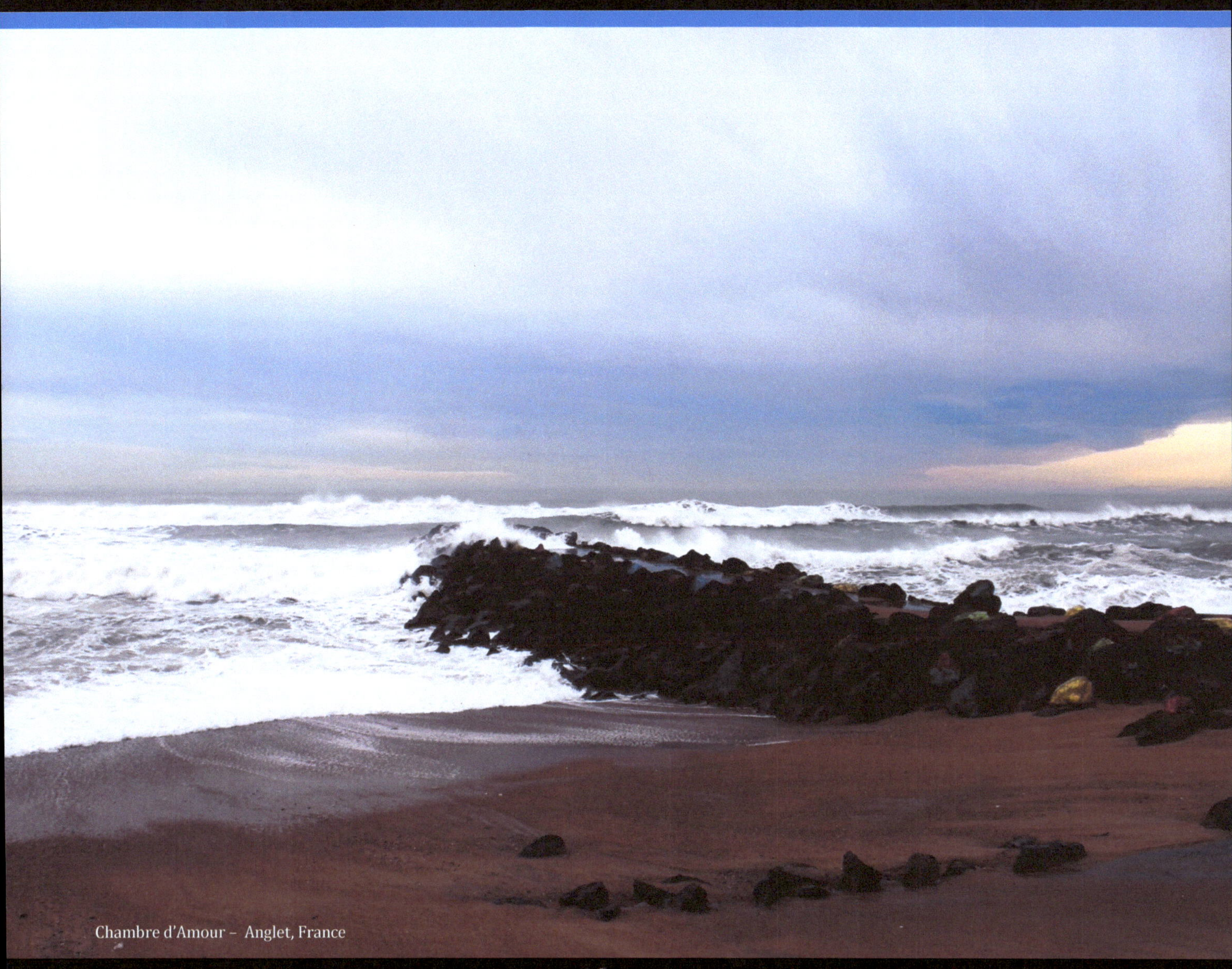

Chambre d'Amour – Anglet, France

I believe in me, and I will create a life that brings me joy

I have the right to be happy. No one can destroy my faith in me.

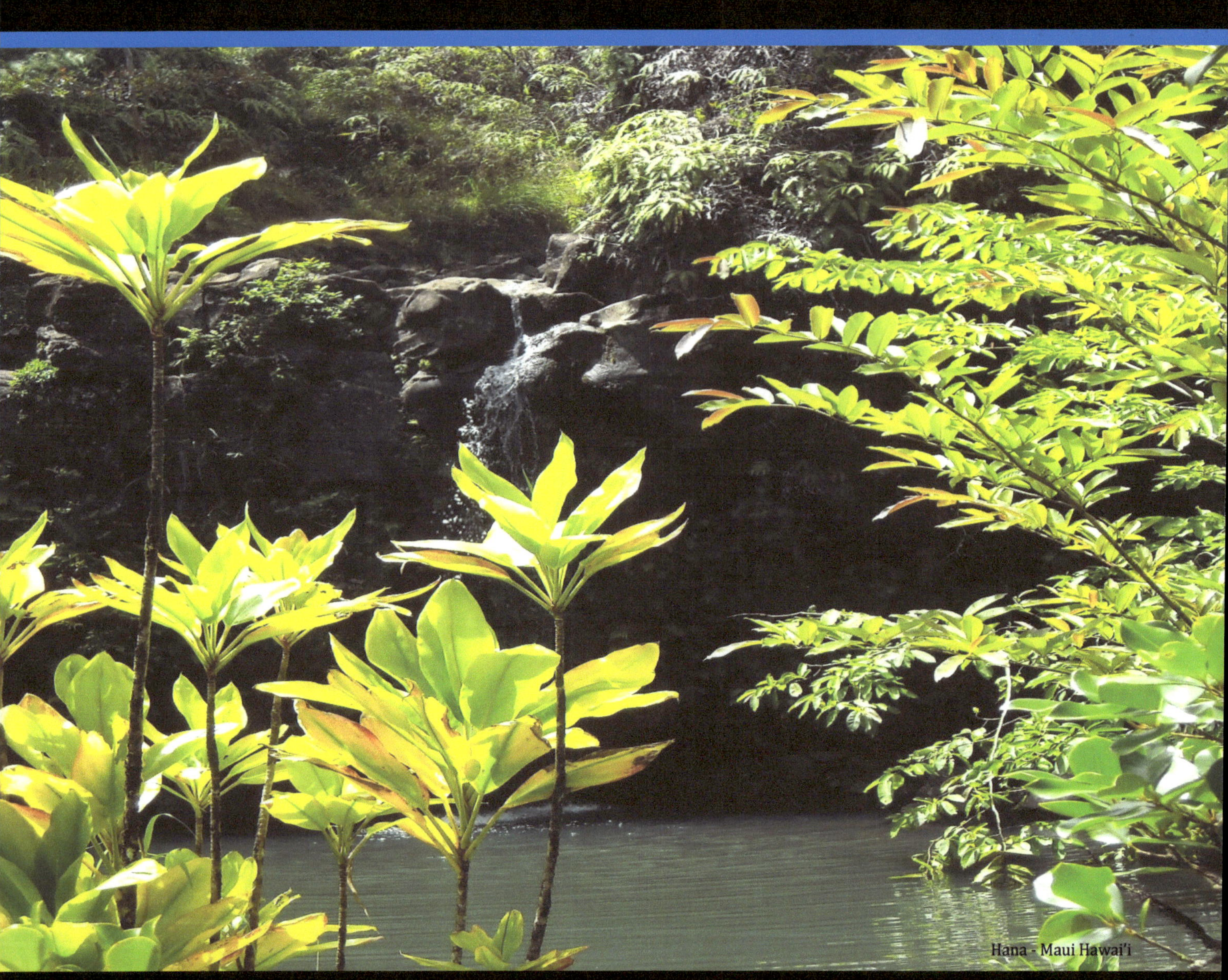

Hana - Maui Hawai'i

I choose to invest in my possibility.

I will not deny my gifts, talents, or abilities.

I believe in me; because I believe in GOD.

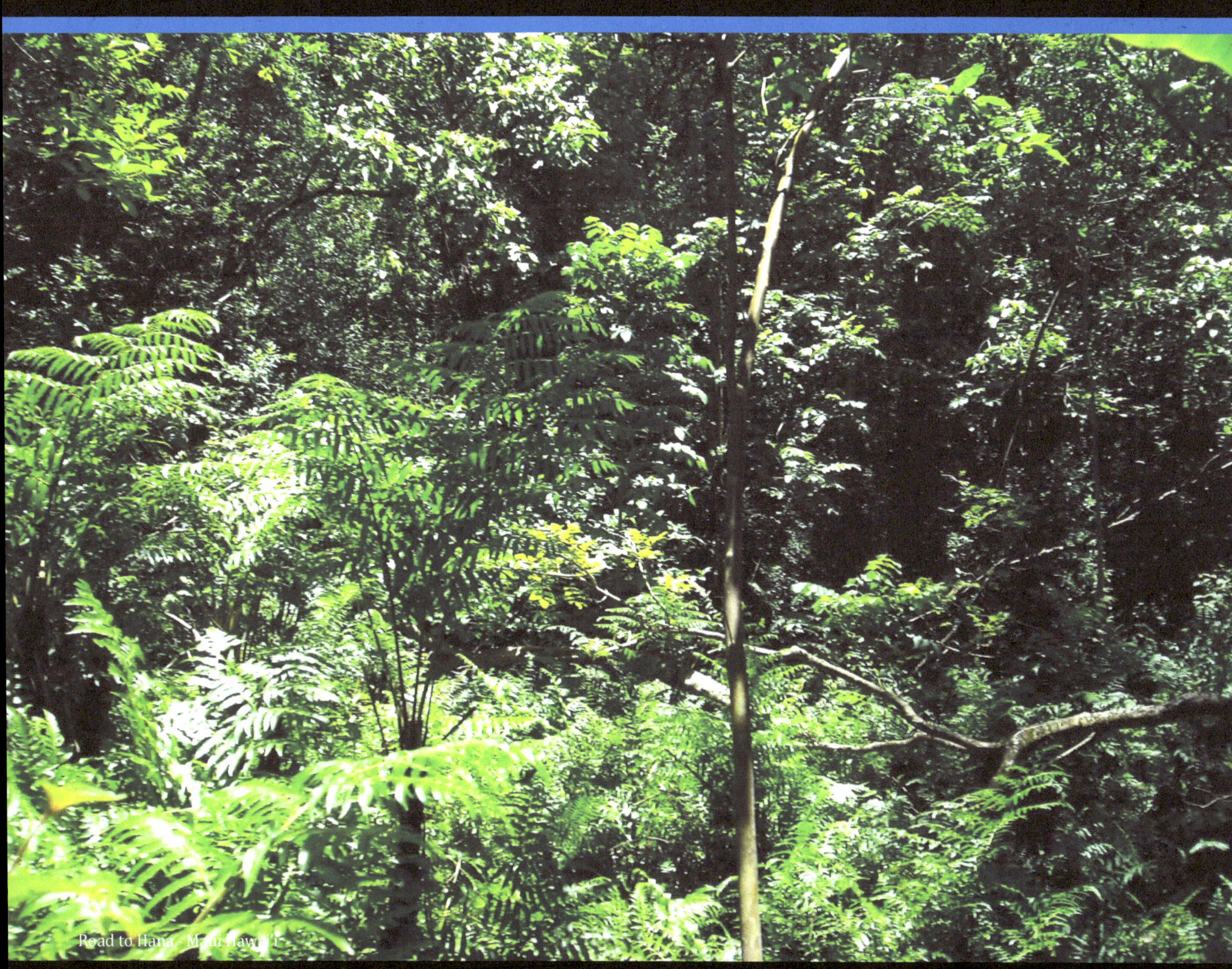

Road to Hana - Maui Hawaii

I choose to embrace all the joy that is possible for me.
I do not look back towards regrets nor forward with any doubt.
Life stands before me and I rejoice.

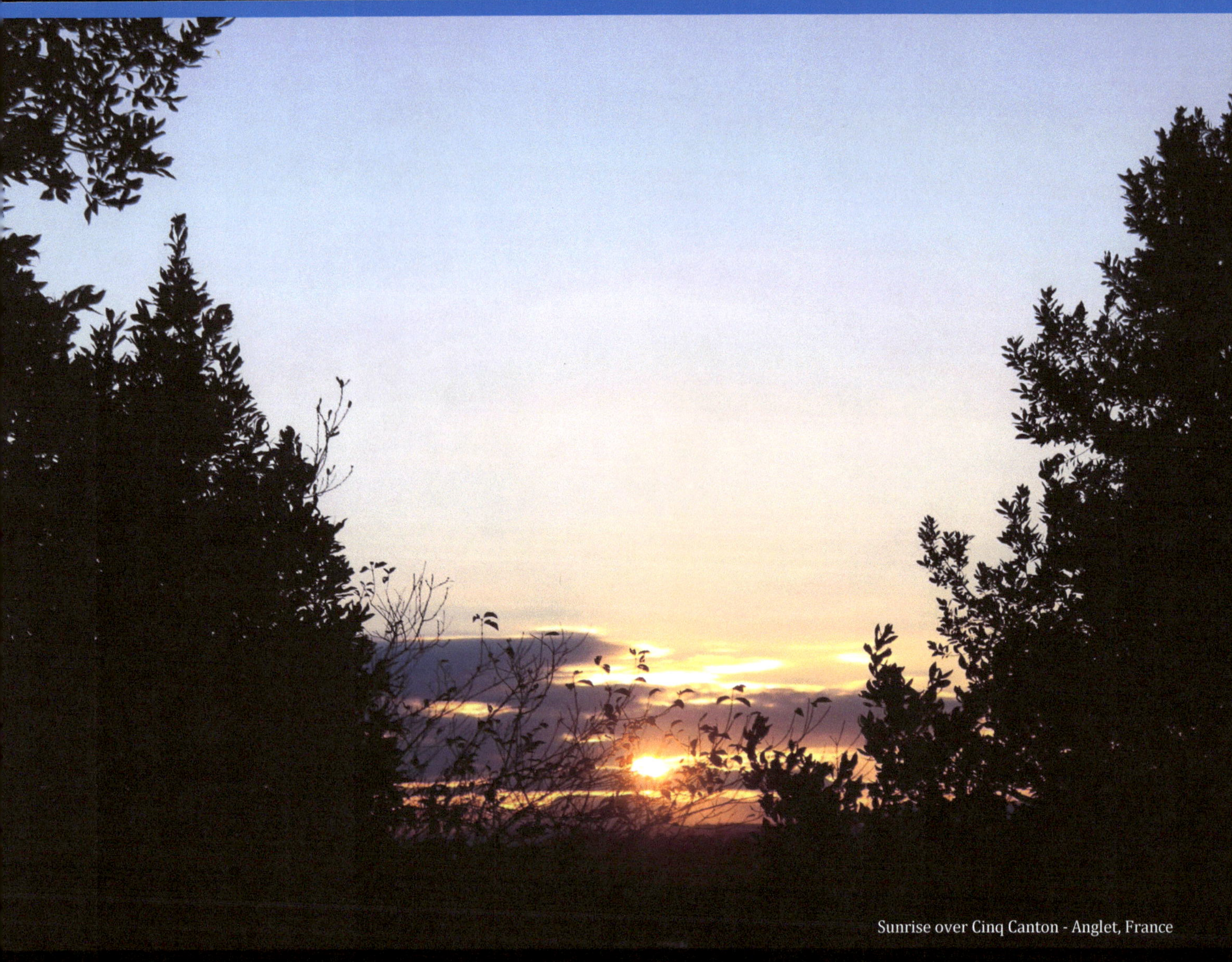

Sunrise over Cinq Canton - Anglet, France

I lay the foundation for my happiness and overcome all adversity.
I have faith in me, and depend on the Divine for everything I need.
I suffer for nothing anymore.

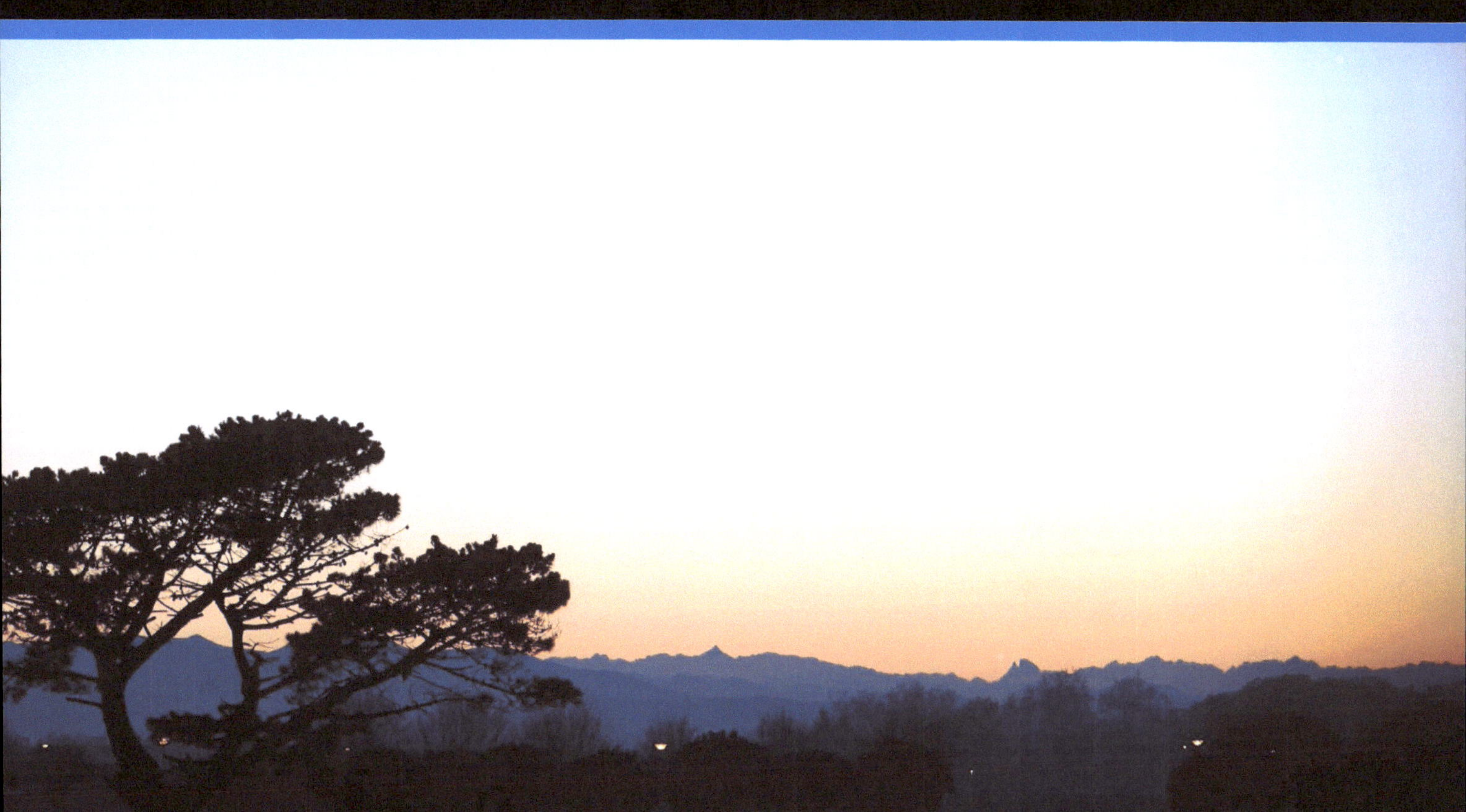

I am never lost. I am following a Divine plan.

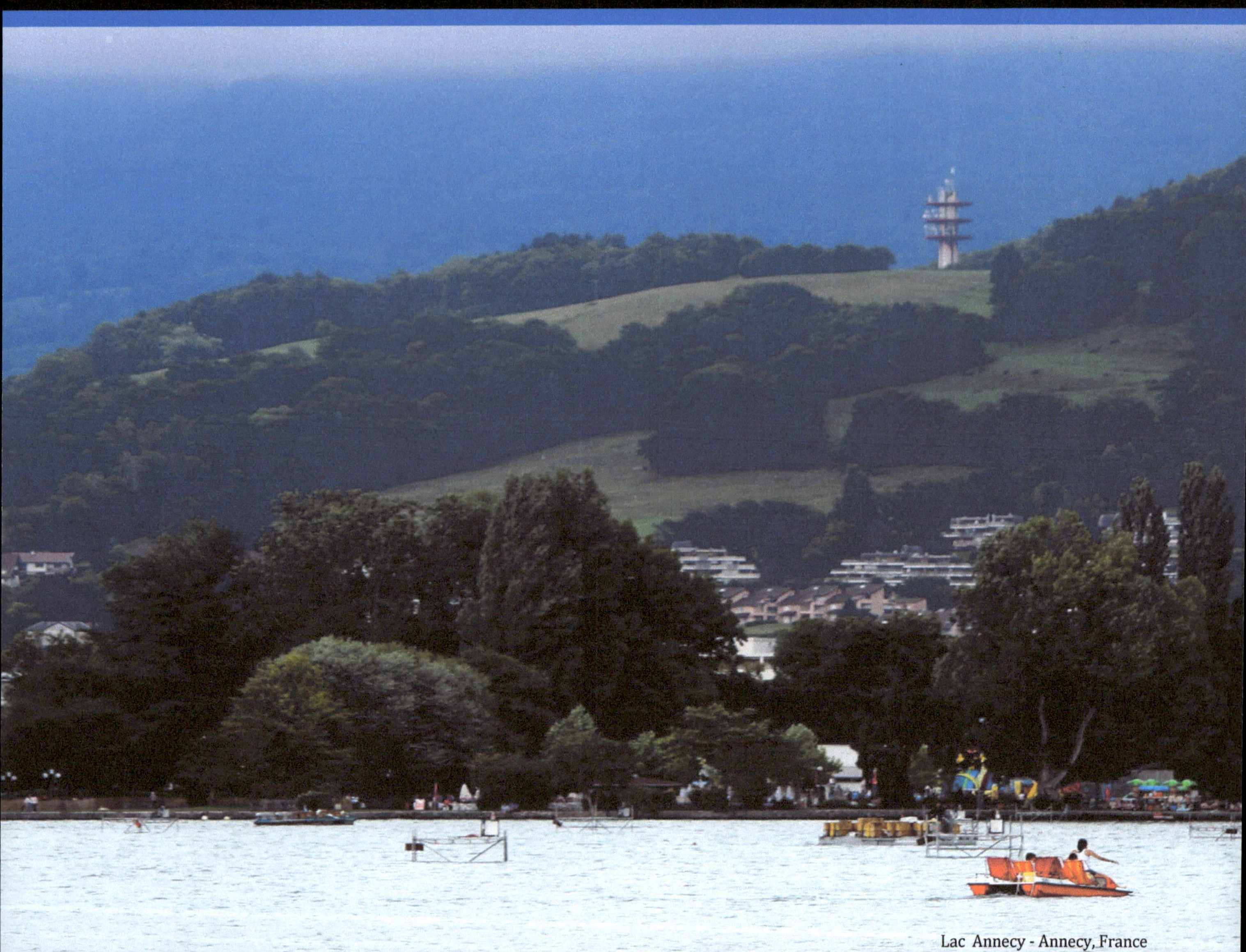

Lac Annecy - Annecy, France

I release my worries to the Divine, so that I am free.
I will do what needs to be done and focus on the now and not the why.

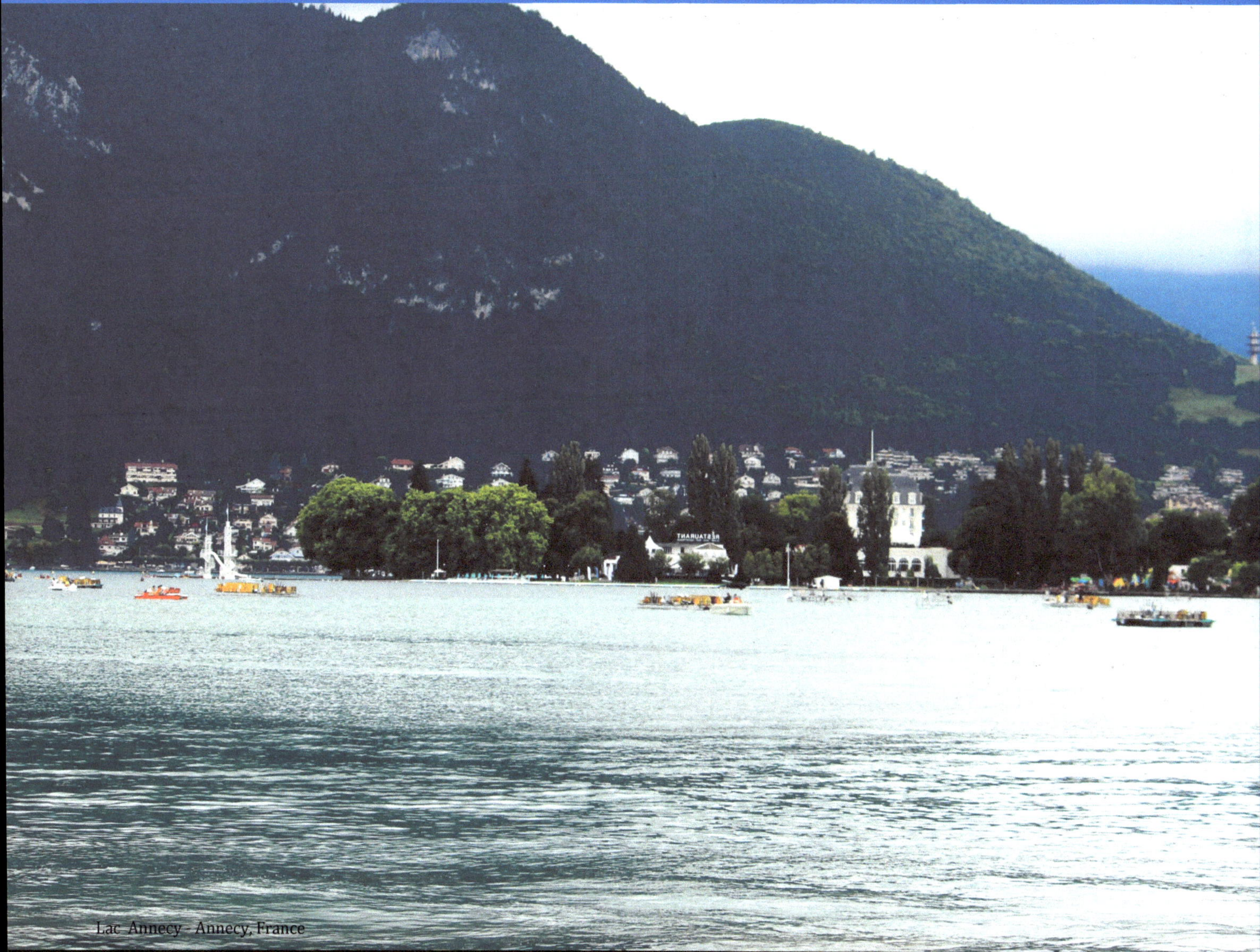

Lac Annecy - Annecy, France

I will rise above all my circumstances.

And I believe in my heart that I shall prevail.

I hope, I act, and I pray.

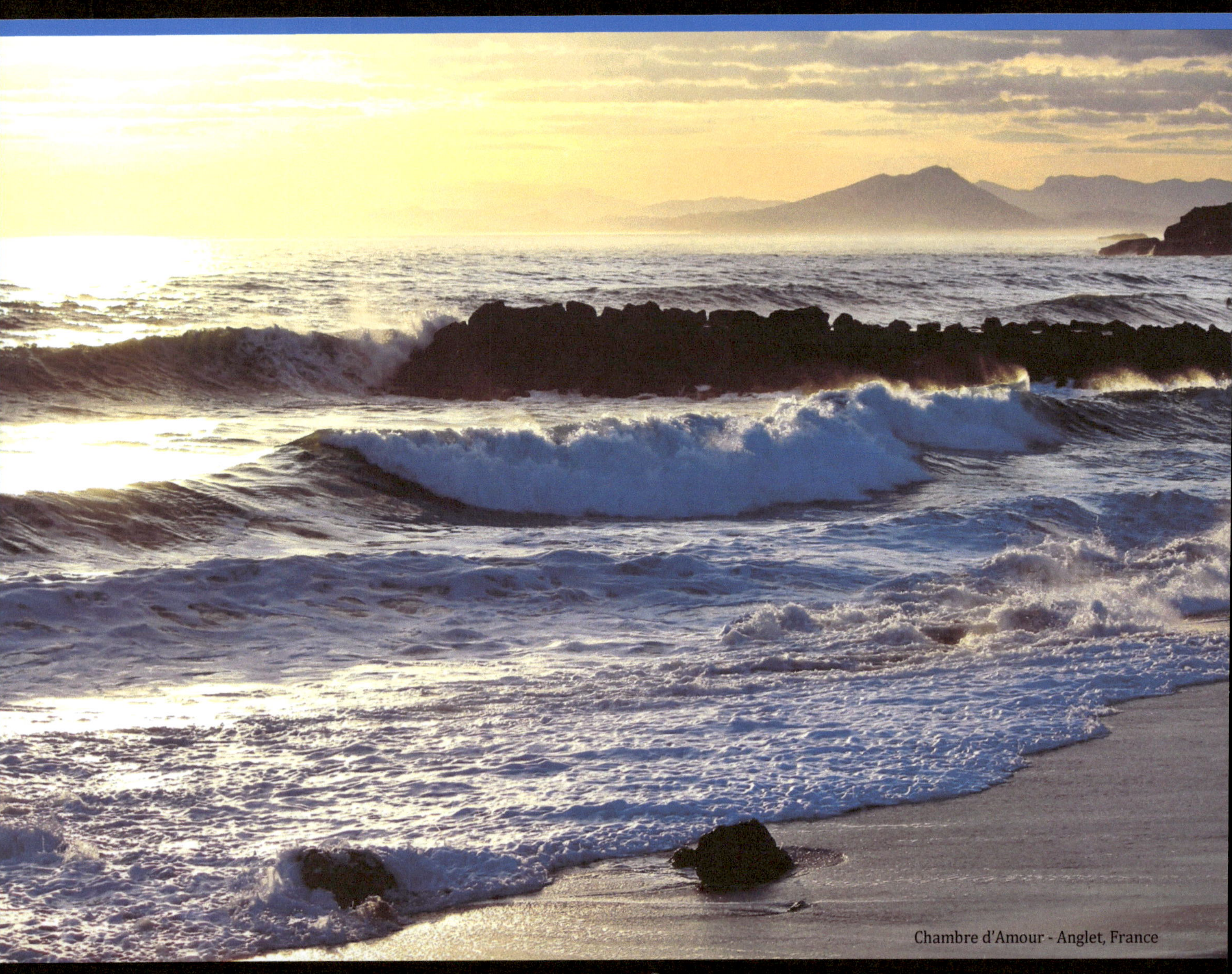

Chambre d'Amour - Anglet, France

I thank GOD for everything I have; every moment I ever laughed and every second I ever loved. For every hug and comfort I have received, and for every kind word or affection shown my way, I am forever grateful.

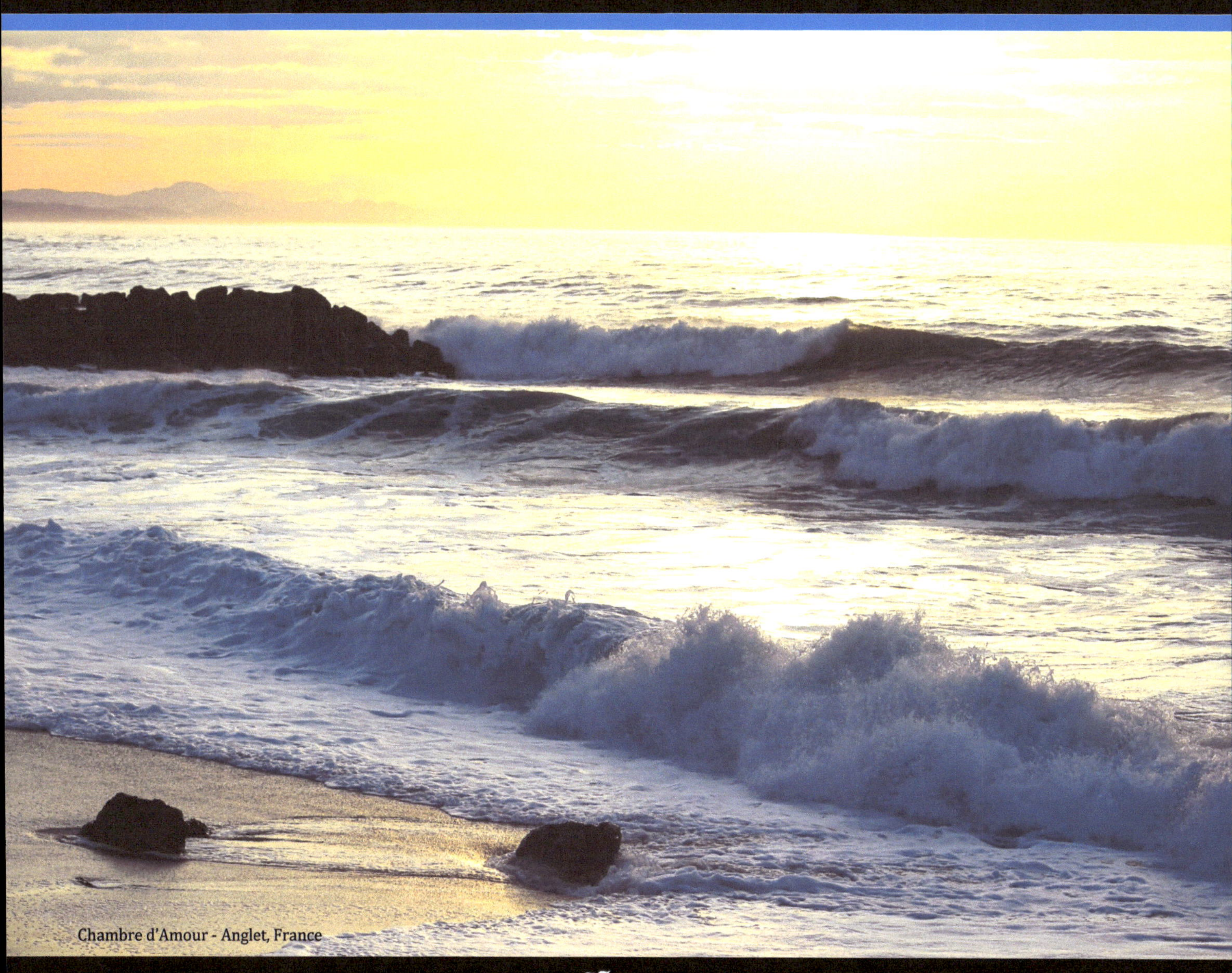

Chambre d'Amour - Anglet, France

I was given the power to make it the day I was born.

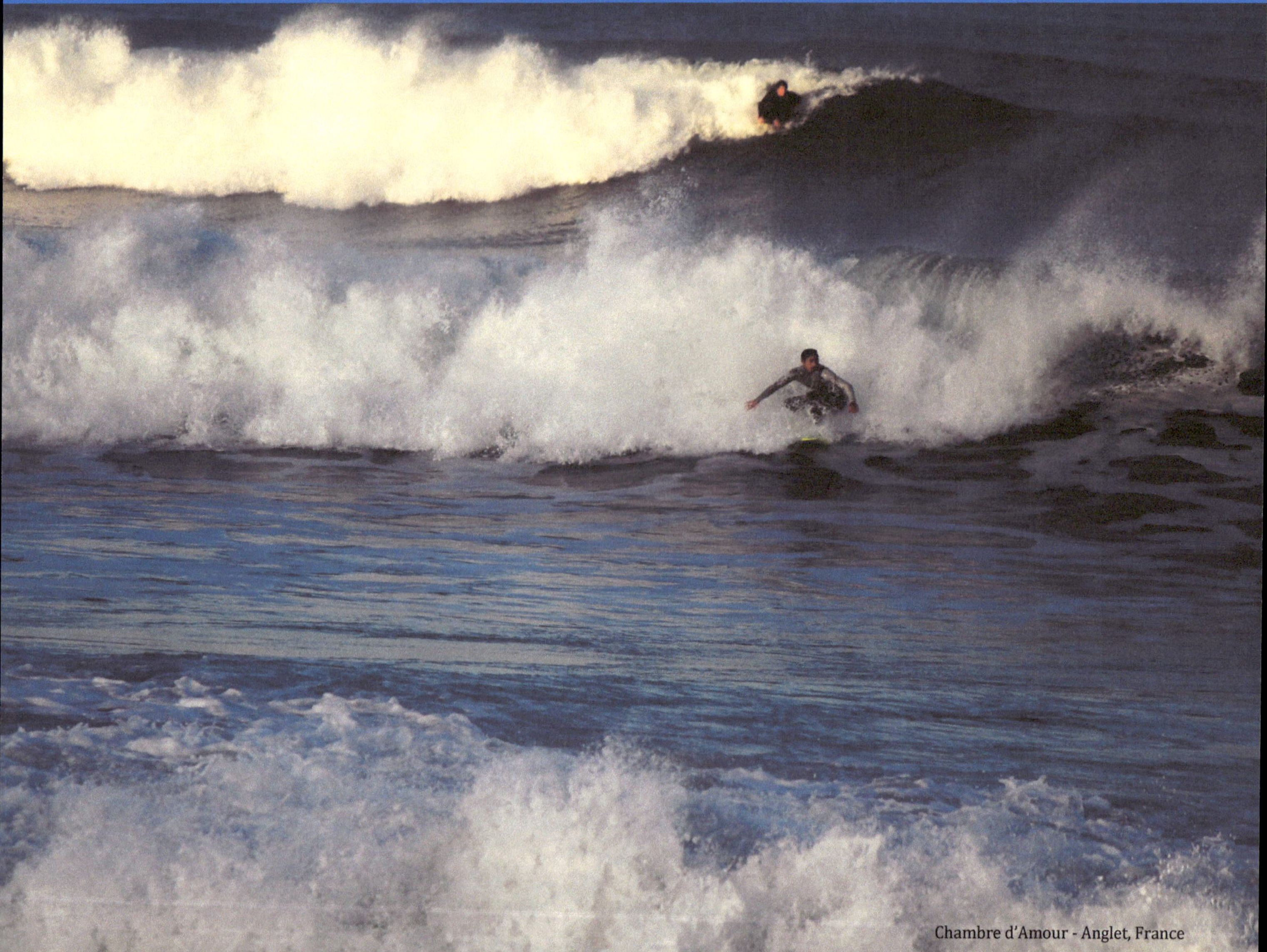

Chambre d'Amour - Anglet, France

Every adversity I face is a testimony to my courage and strength.

And every hardship I endure only makes me stronger.

I am holding on to the hand of GOD, and faith shall guide me and give me the courage to stand.

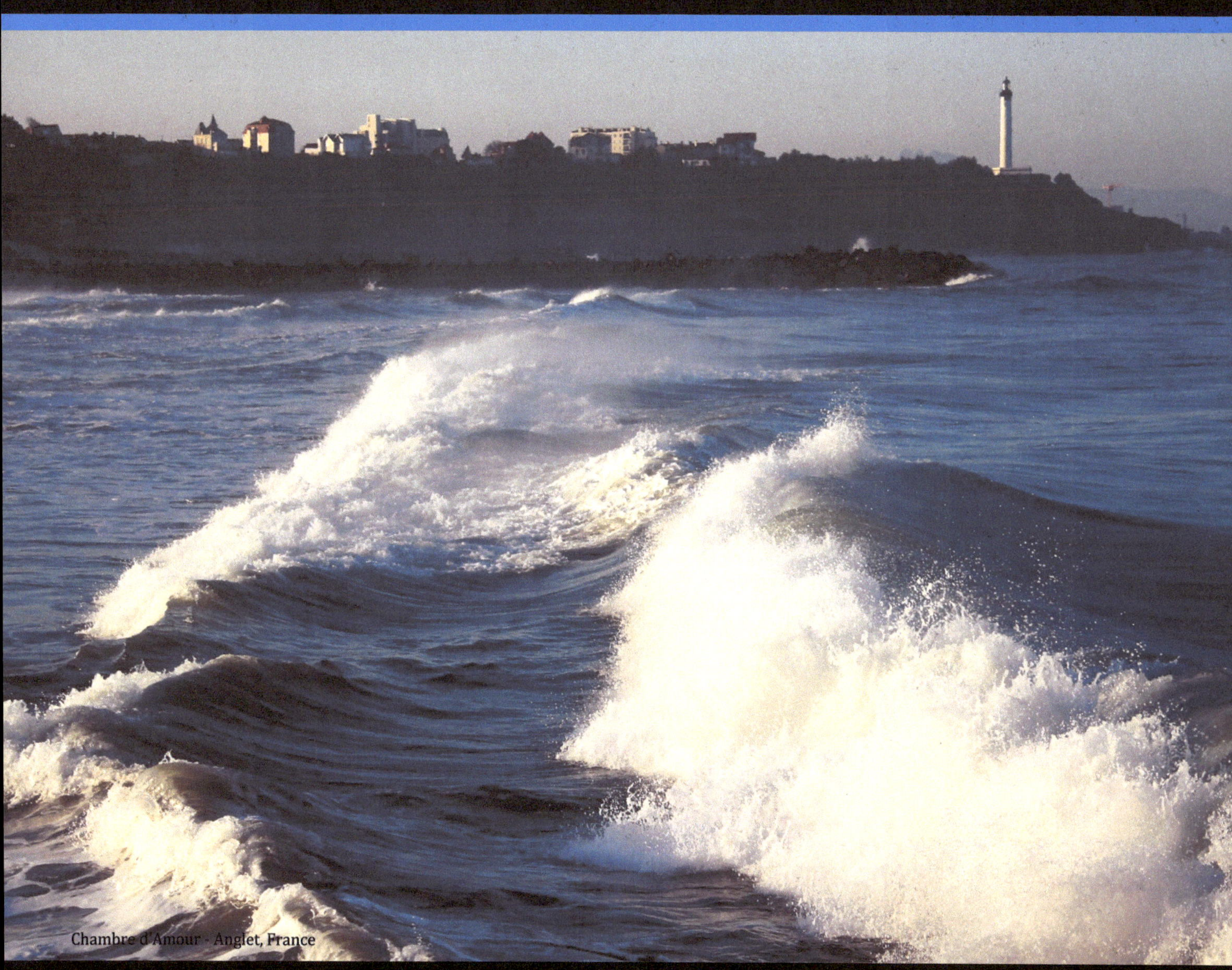

Chambre d'Amour - Anglet, France

I trust myself, because I trust in GOD.

I have been taught right from wrong and will judge my road accordingly.

I will follow the signs left before me, and above all, I will be wise.

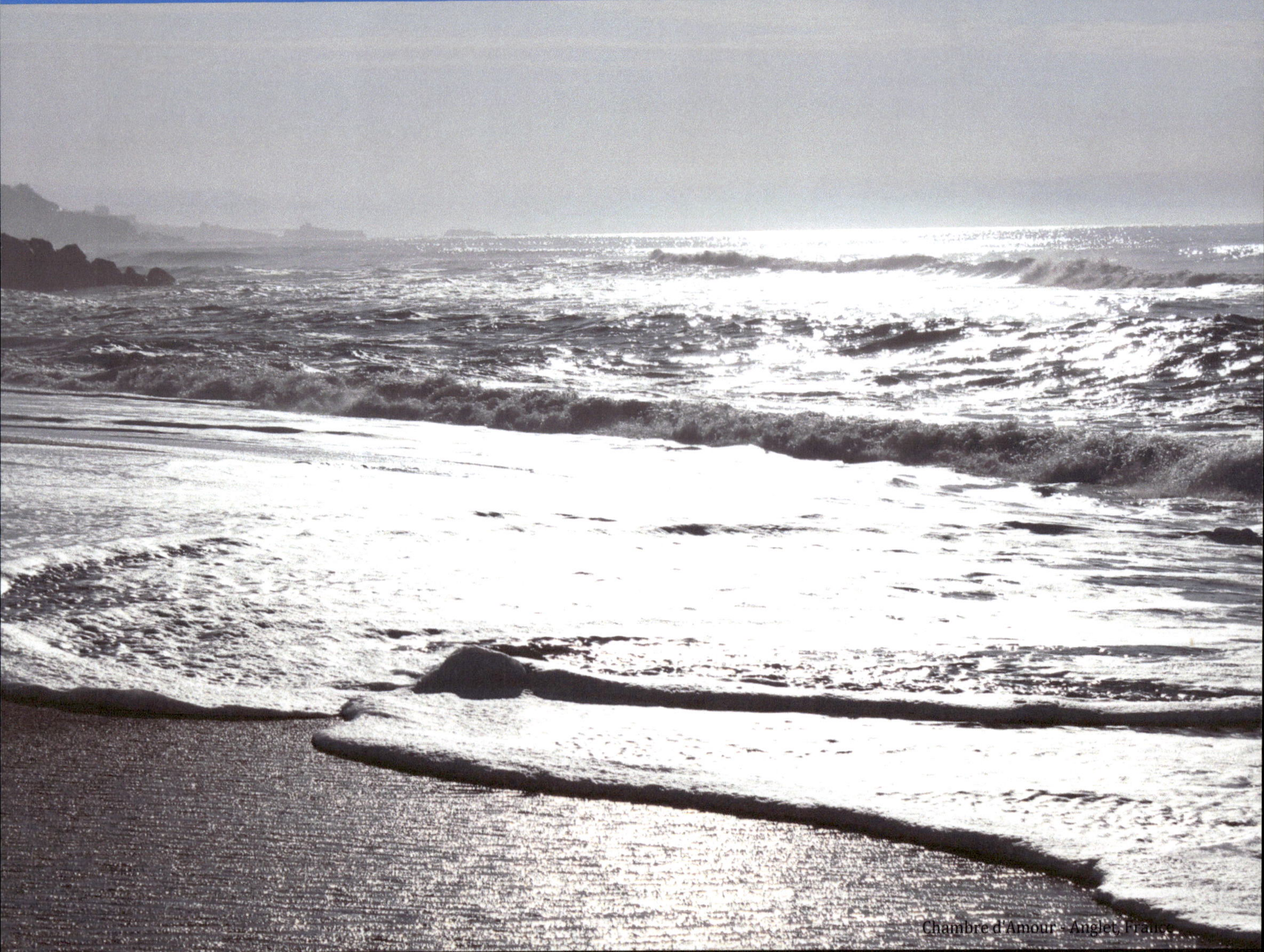

Chambre d'Amour - Anglet, France

I choose what I give my power to.

I choose to focus on what is good, what is loving, what is prosperous, and what brings me joy. I will no longer allow worry to enter my mind.

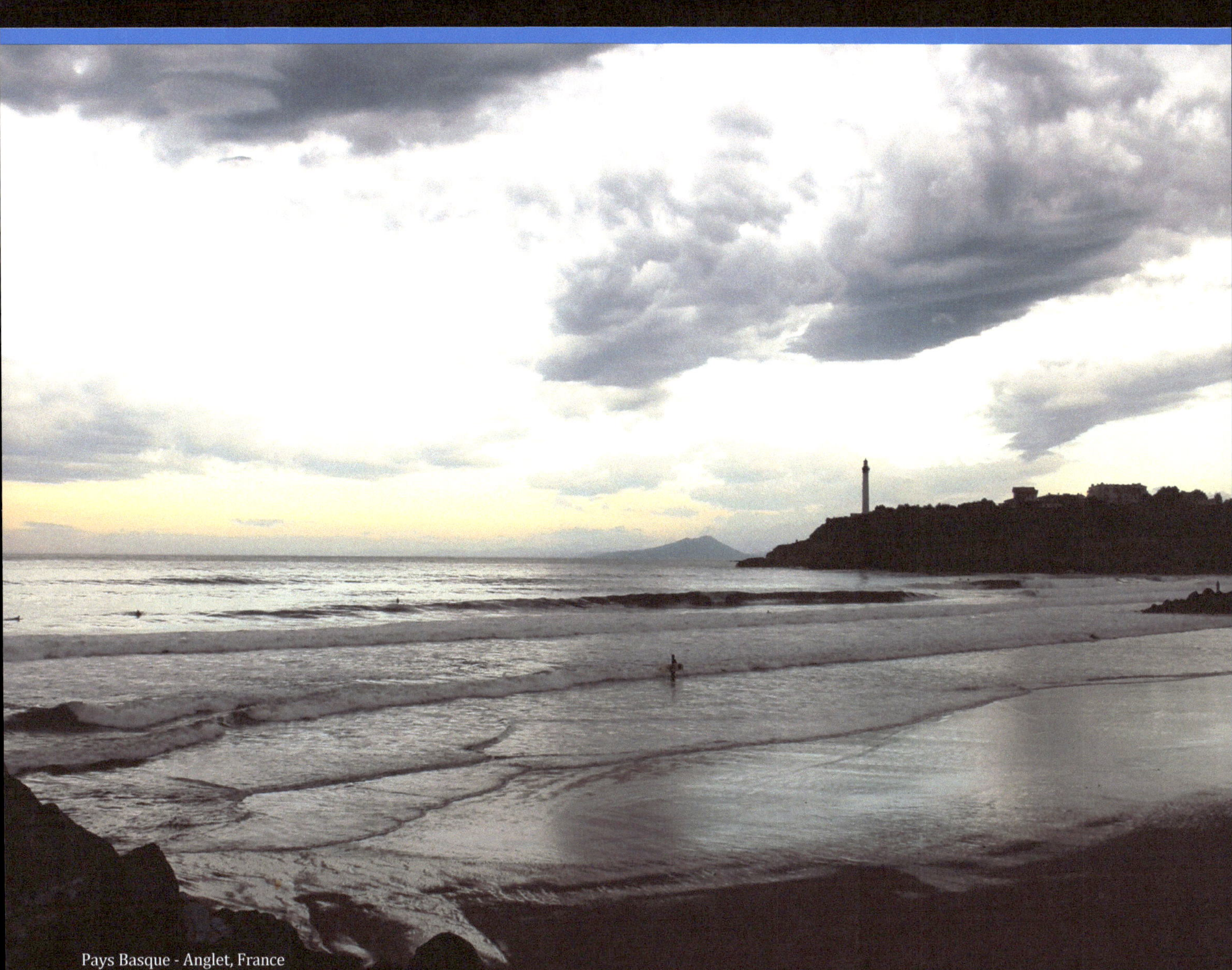

Pays Basque - Anglet, France

It is my Divine right to live my dreams and I claim them without fear.

I believe in them. I will work for them, and they are mine.

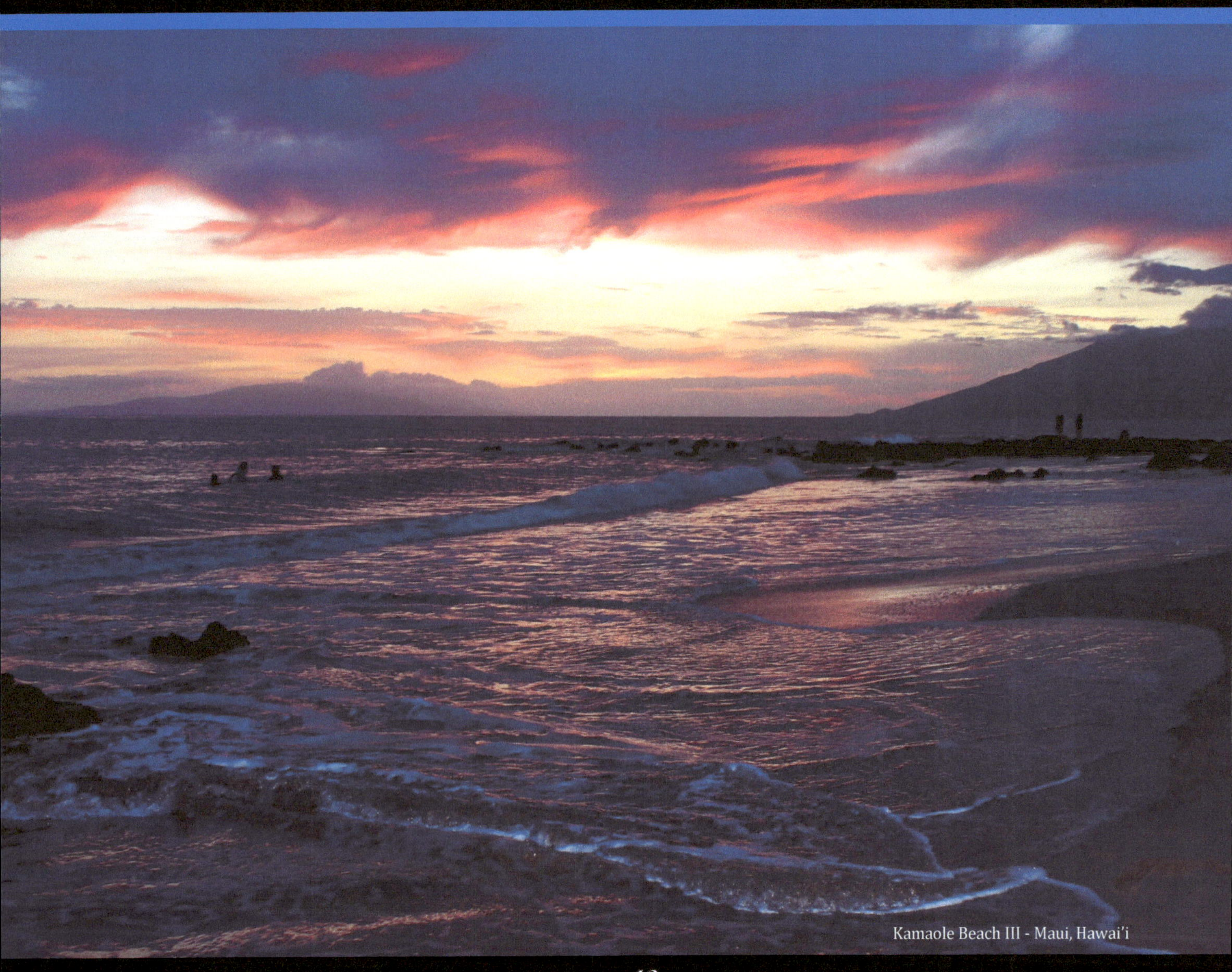

Kamaole Beach III - Maui, Hawai'i

I will triumph despite what has happened in my life.
I know that all trials come to make me strong, and I am strong.
I can smile, because I live. I refuse to be brought down. I refuse to be stepped on,
disrespected, or abused. I let go of all the things that cause me pain. I shall be in peace.

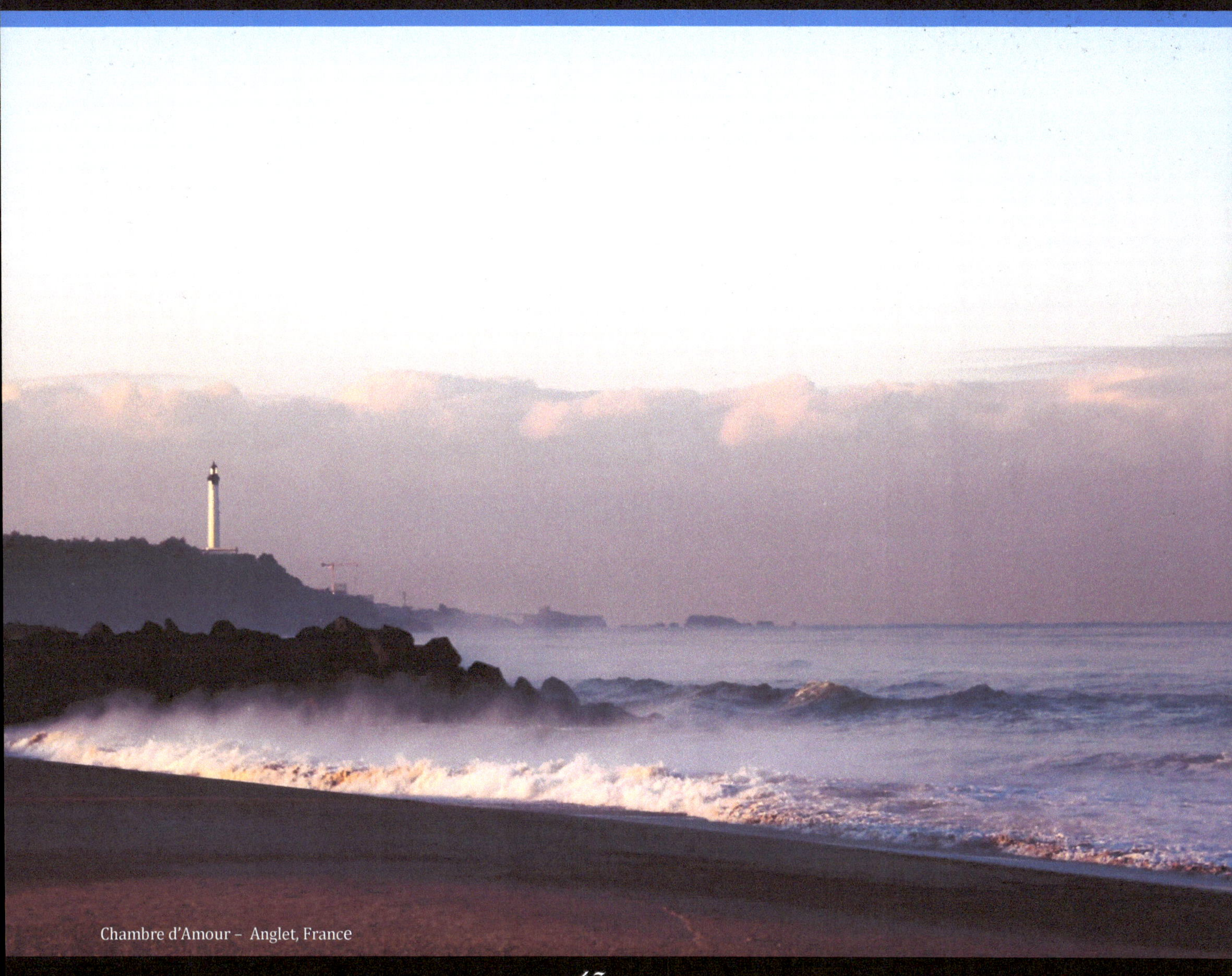

Chambre d'Amour – Anglet, France

The power to manifest is within me...

I claim it. I believe it. I have it. It is done.

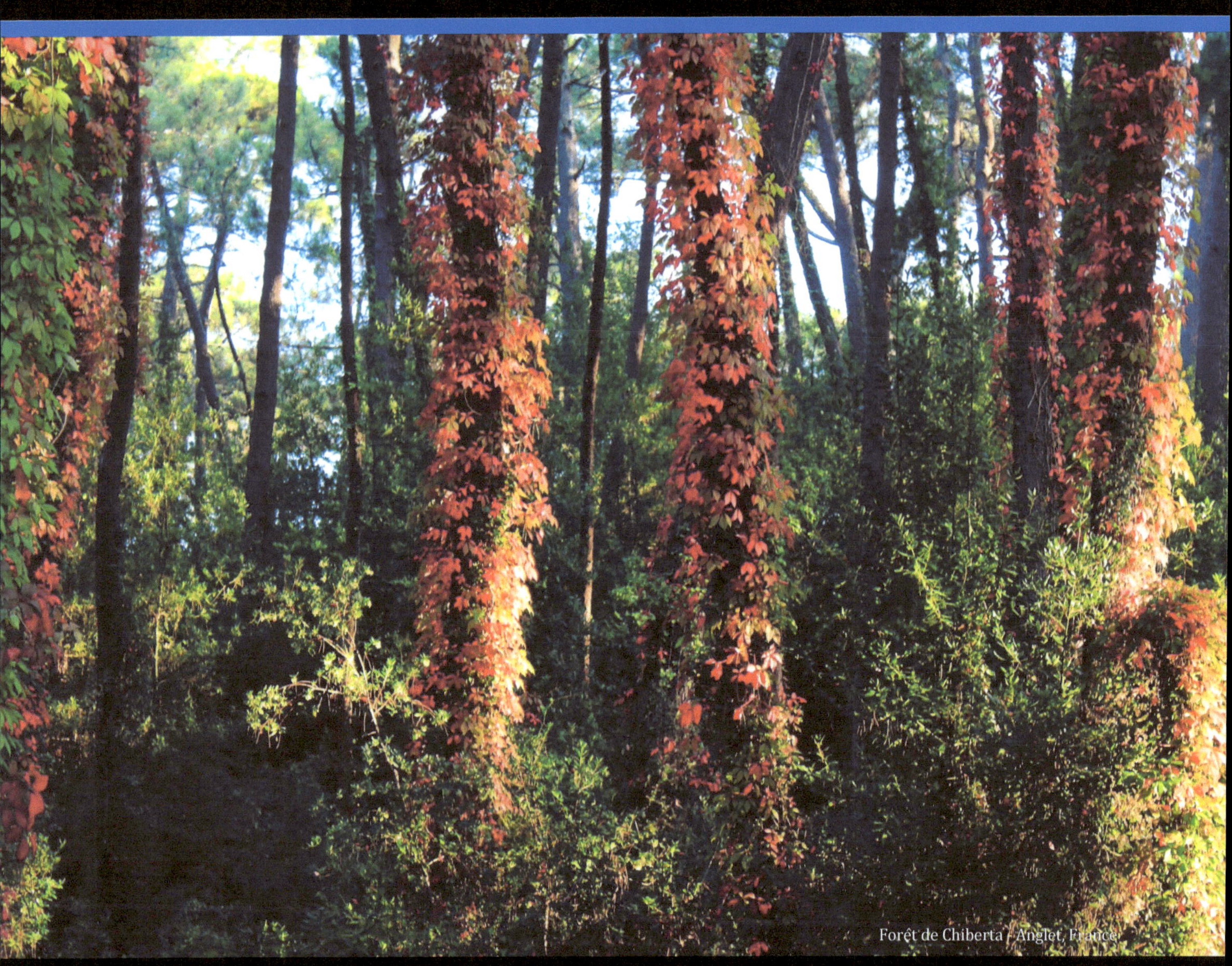

Forêt de Chiberta - Anglet, France

Everything that I have lived, I have already overcome. There is nothing that I have done that the Divine has not already forgiven me for because I am deeply loved. And because of this, I will not be defeated,nor will I grieve. I will be strong.

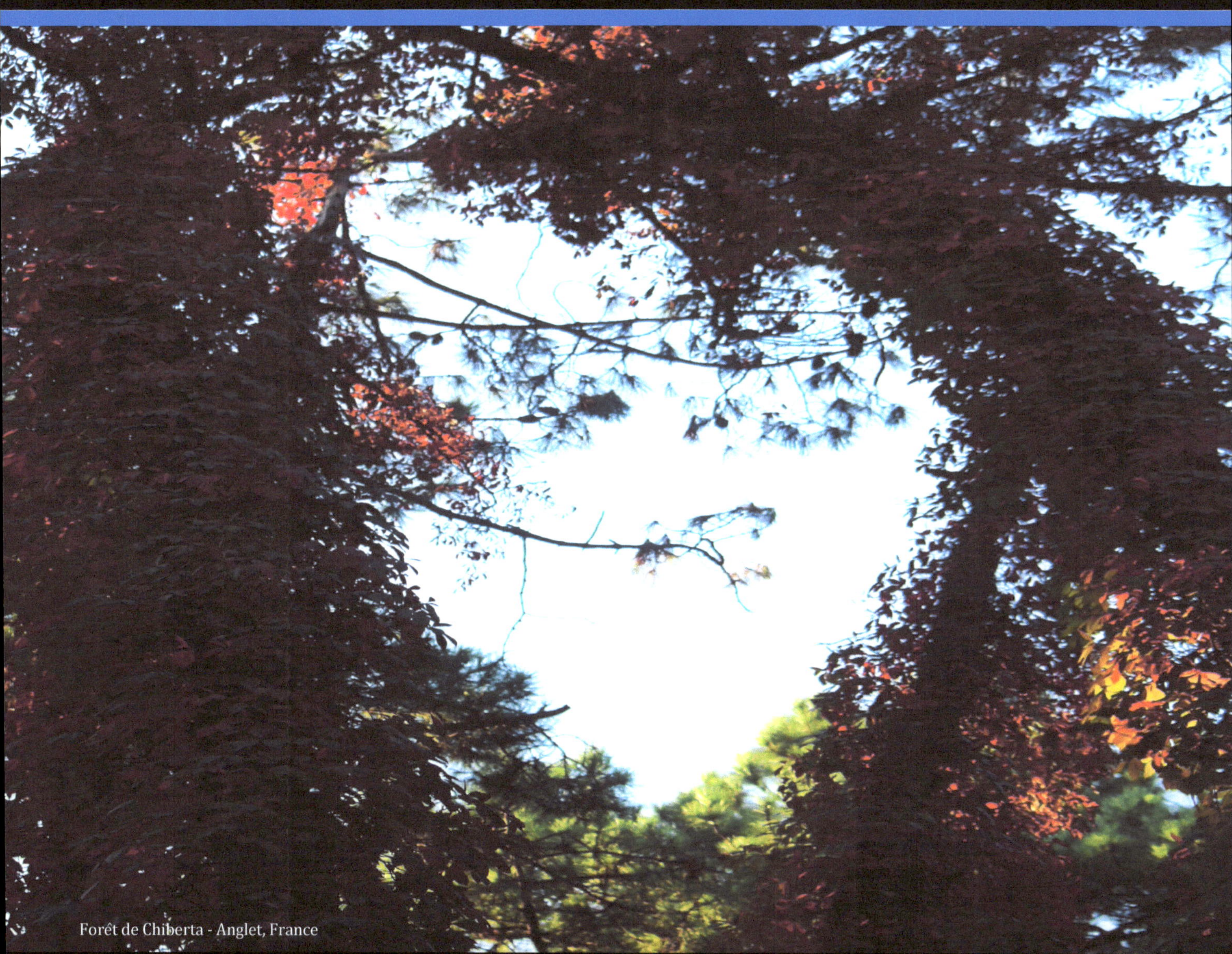

Forêt de Chiberta - Anglet, France

I will live my life according to what is right for me.

I am determined to be happy, to be prosperous, generous, loving, and kind.

I am determined to be me.

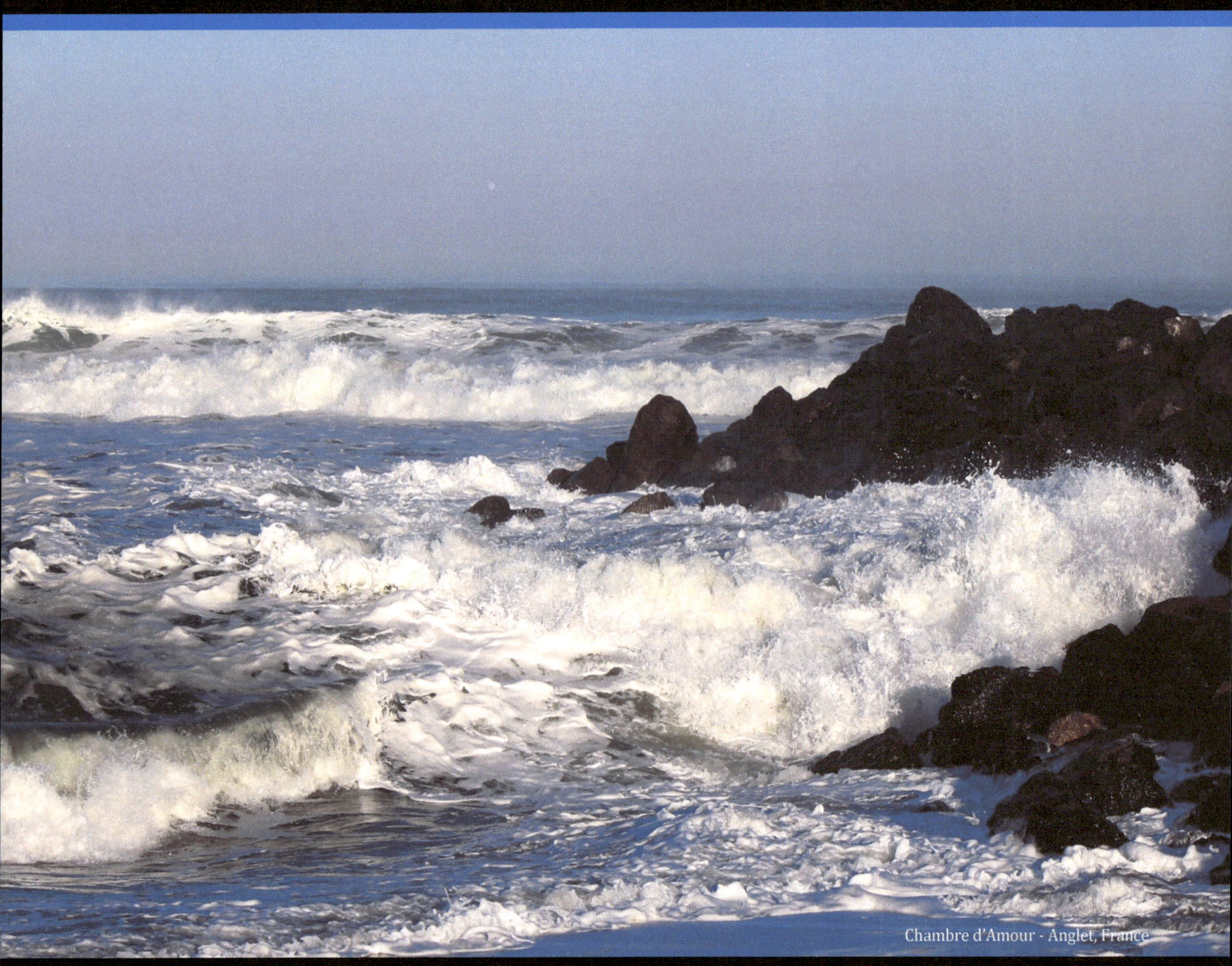

Chambre d'Amour - Anglet, France

My worth is not determined by how much I own or I much I owe. Nor is it diminished by broken heart, a disappointment, or loss. My worth is completely Divinely given and cannot be taken away. I am as precious as life itself.

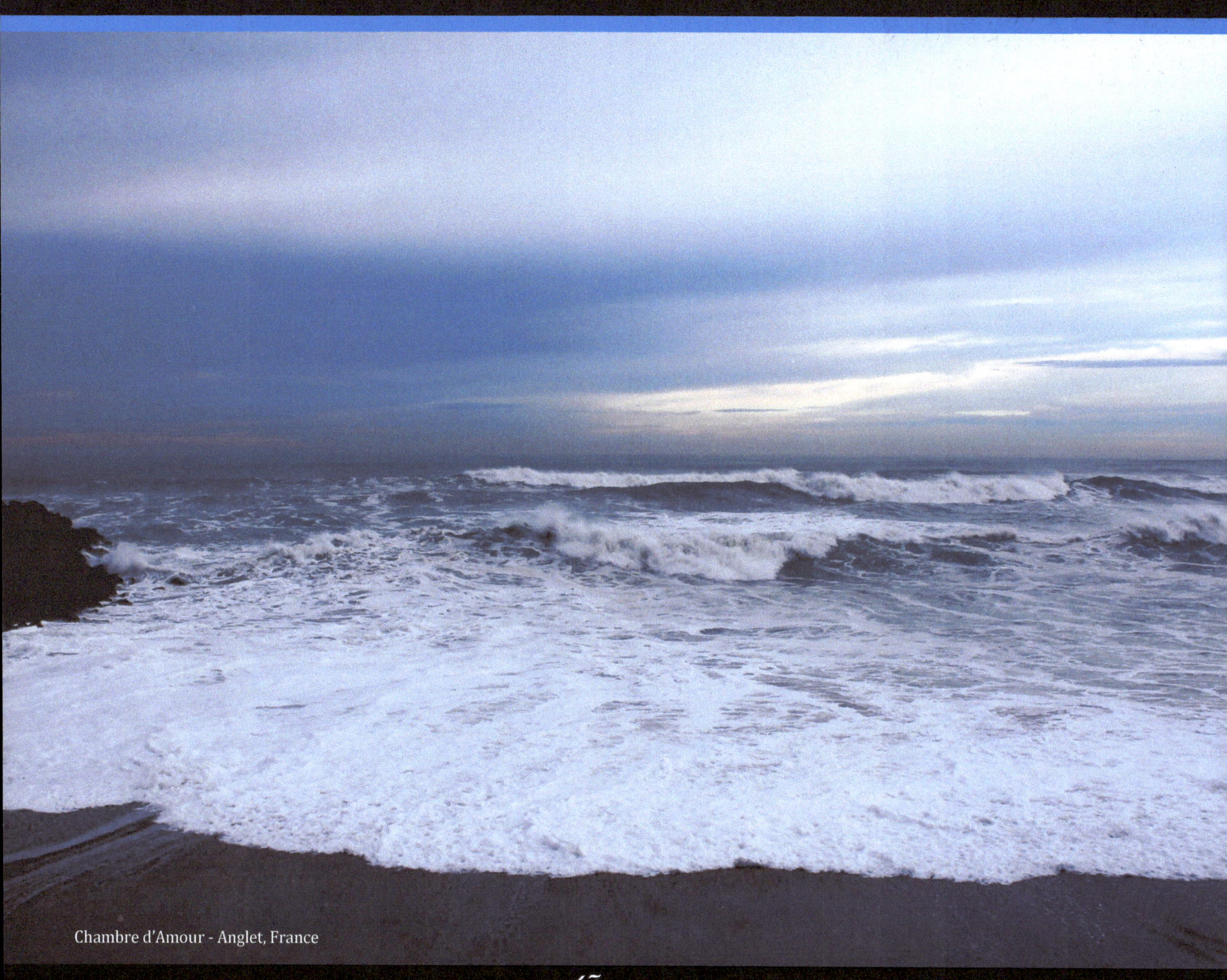

Chambre d'Amour - Anglet, France

If they speak to me with unkind words, or accuse me to break my heart. I will not listen.

There is nothing they can say to me that will bring me down.

I stand tall in the face of adversity for I know who I am. And I am worthy of love.

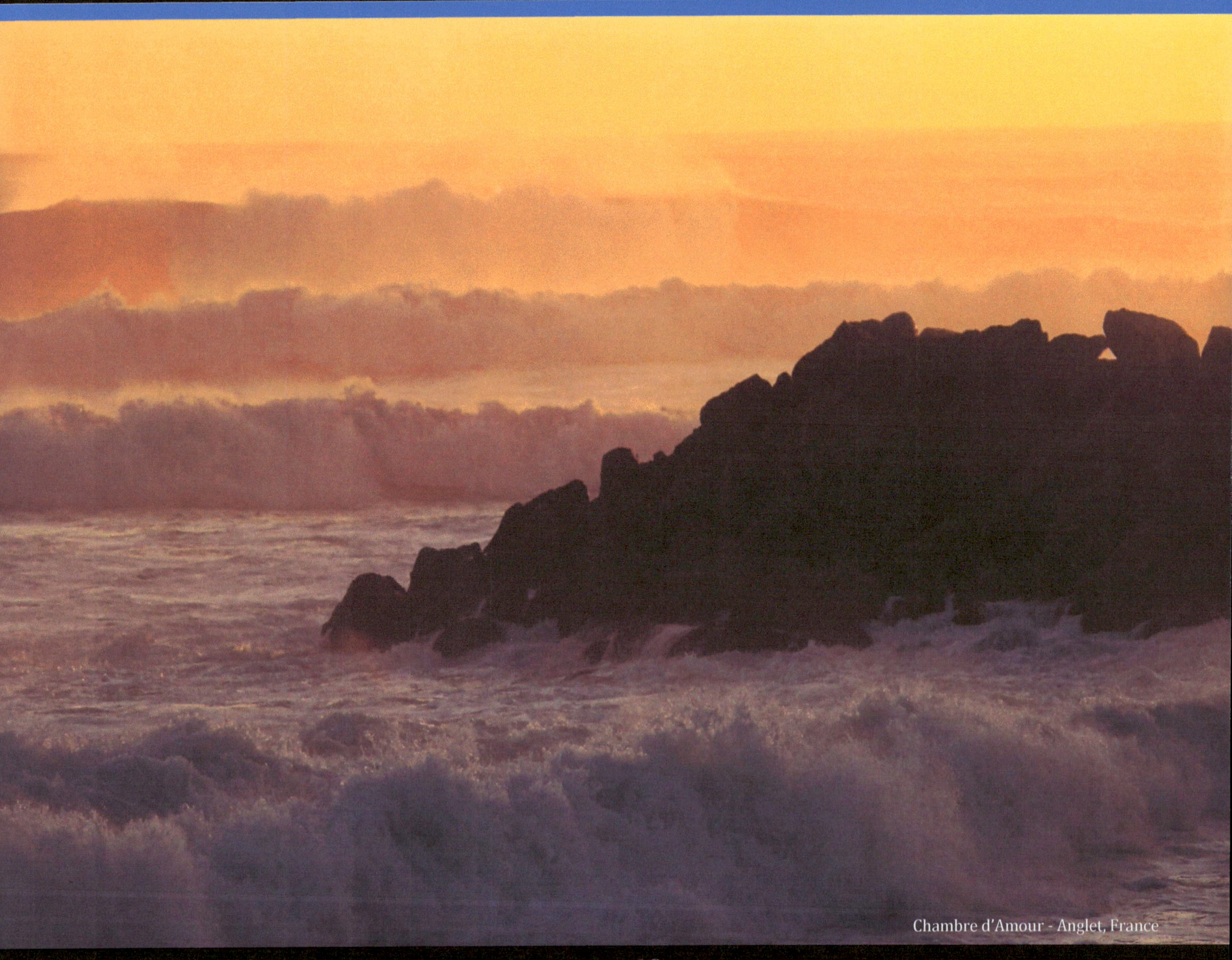

Chambre d'Amour - Anglet, France

I will lift my head and live and my faith shall not be shaken

for the Lord GOD is with me and I am very much alive.

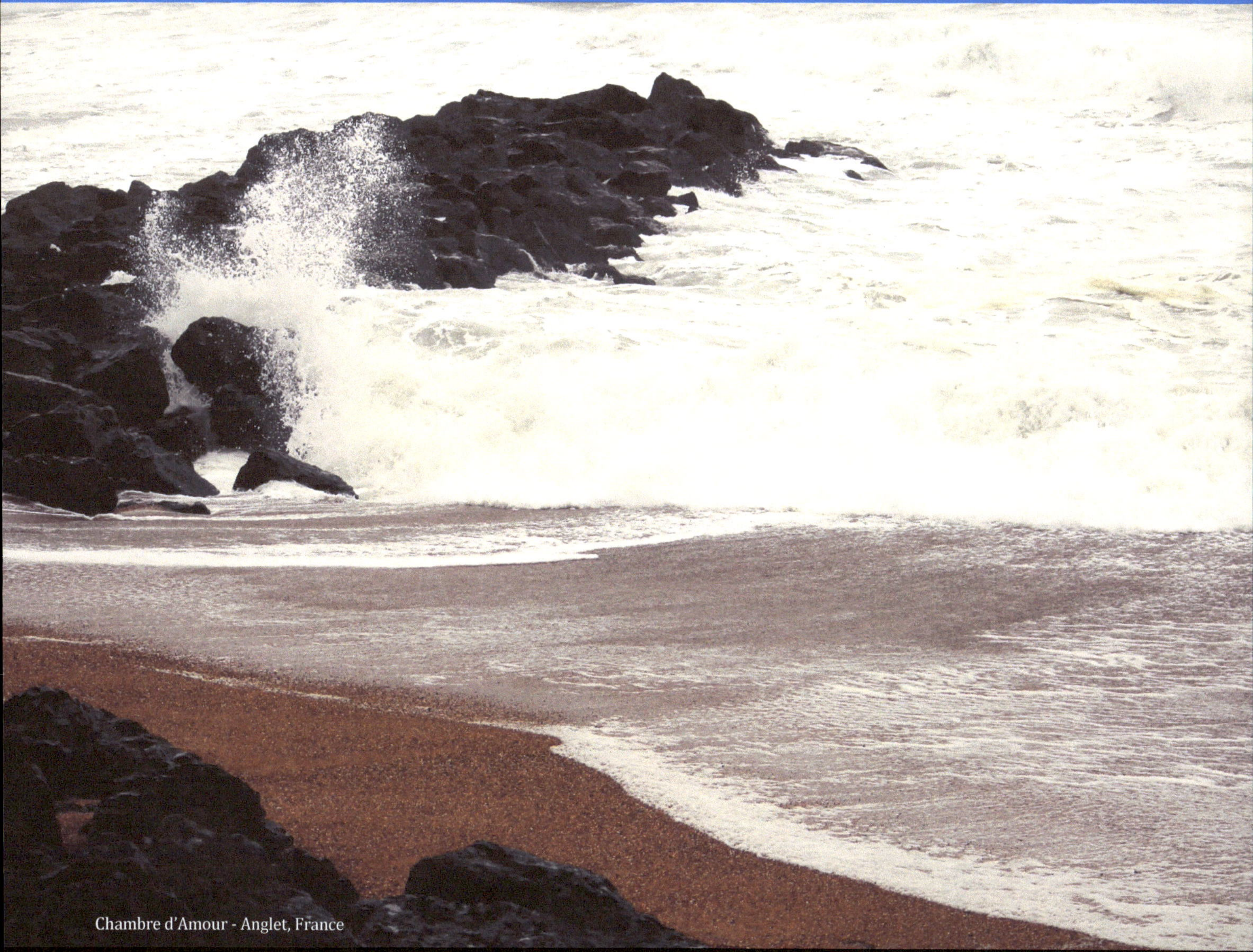

Chambre d'Amour - Anglet, France

If I can inspire a heart to beat again, or breathe life into a dream;
hearten those who cry in the night and bring them the morning sun,
then my journey was worth the tears, and I triumphed in the midst of them all.

-D. Ashanti-Dubois

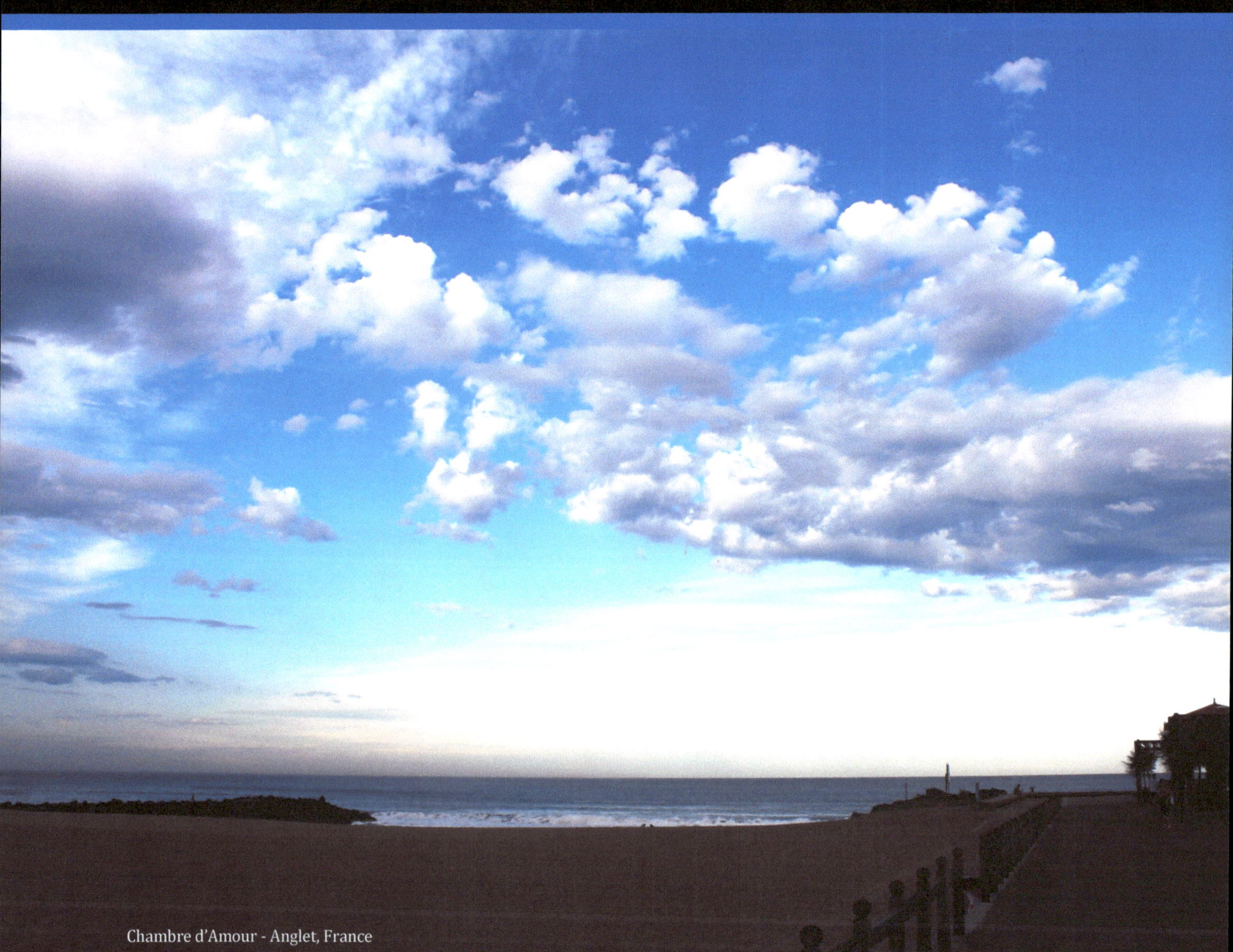

Chambre d'Amour - Anglet, France

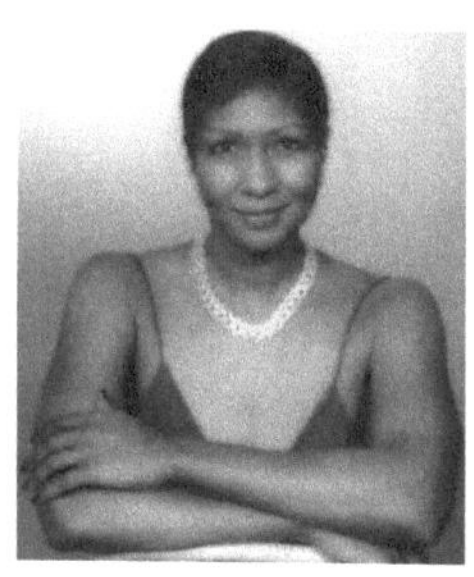

ABOUT THE AUTHOR

Author and creative artist, D. Ashanti-Dubois, brings light and love to the universe of literature through her latest edition, Messages of Hope - Affirmations to Empower Your Life. As a multifaceted writer, photographer, vocalist, composer, graphic artist, and inspirational speaker, D. Ashanti-Dubois brings a unique perspective to the world of spiritual enlightenment. After nearly two decades of living internationally and in Hawaii, her intrepid journey has emboldened her belief in the spirit of hope, love, and humanity.

Born and raised in St. Louis, Missouri where she began her creative journey writing poetry, prose, and songs at the tender age of five, D. Ashanti-Dubois continues her artistic odyssey producing various genres of books, music, photography, and art.

Her spiritual anthology, *Messages of Hope,* is a collection of beautifully written spiritual insights to inspire and empower your life. The entire Messages of Hope series can be purchased online through Amazon.com and other vendors. Also available: *Messages of Hope – Words to Uplift the Human Spirit Special Edition:* An uplifting book of 33 inspirational messages and 40 exercises to change in your life along with more than 200 gorgeous original photographs. *Messages d'Amour–Reflections of Love:* A romantic diary of love poems with gorgeous floral photography to inspire love and romance. *Heaven & Earth:* A magnificent collection of spiritual poetry and nature photography.

For more books available by D. Ashanti-Dubois visit www.mydovesong.com. Look for other editions scheduled to be released in the coming years.

www.ingramcontent.com/pod-product-compliance
Lightning Source LLC
LaVergne TN
LVHW070152110826
845147LV00002B/378
* 9 7 8 0 6 1 5 9 7 7 8 2 9 *